I0150825

Finding Joy

My Journey Begins

Jo Moffatt

Jo Moffatt

This book is dedicated to my wonderful brother Ted. He has taught me that true success is embracing life with love and joy.

Acknowledgements

I would like to thank a number of people who have helped immensely with the creation and fine tuning of this book. Thank you Laurie, Jerry and Brenda for your encouragement and helpful suggestions. A special thanks to Jill for allowing me to hear my words. Your help and enthusiasm has been invaluable to me. Thank you Gil for all your patience and support and thank you Laura for both your personal and professional encouragement as well as your technical help. Another special thanks goes to Stephanie Rowe for her incredible talent in designing my book cover. I would also like to express my appreciation for my copy editor Sherry Hinman. She cleaned my story while leaving my *voice* intact. And most of all, I would like to thank Abraham for helping me to reconnect with William. Without that reconnection, this book would not exist. If you are interested in learning more about the teachings of Abraham, I encourage you to read Esther & Jerry Hicks story on the official Abraham-Hicks website at:

www.abraham-hicks.com

Jo Moffatt

Chapter 1

I got up from the kitchen table, scooping up my journal and pen, and headed toward the hall. I switched on the overhead light in the hall and went back in the kitchen to turn off the main light, leaving the dim glow of the stove light on. As I headed down the still unfamiliar hall toward my bedroom, I could hear the muffled sounds of the television coming from the basement. The distant sound was somehow comforting. When I reached my bedroom door, I opened it, flipped on the light switch and went back down the hall to turn off the other light. Making my next trip down the hall, I heard laughter coming from the basement.

Oh, good. They're watching a comedy. Maybe they'll stay up later tonight. I'll have a much better chance of being asleep before they come to bed. It's funny how, even after all this time, I'm still afraid to be the last person to fall asleep. I closed my door, walked over to the side of my bed and turned on the small bedside lamp. Then back to the door to shut off the overhead light. The routine was the same every night. Different house, same routine.

The darkness still scares me. I wonder if it will always be this way—if I will ever feel comfortable in the dark again. I quickly changed into my pyjamas and got in under the covers.

I was feeling a little excited about the next day. The anticipation was exhilarating. I was nervous, though. *What will it be like?* As I lay there with the blankets snuggled up under my chin, I looked around my new room, illuminated only by the soft glow of my small bedside lamp.

I loved my new room. In fact, I loved my new home. It was so much larger than the one I had grown up in for most of my life. It was more like the house I'd lived in for the first six years of my life. *Was I only six years old the last time I moved? Yes, that's right. Wow, it seems like it was a lifetime ago. So much has happened. I'm not even the same person anymore. Not really. But this move is my big chance for a fresh start.*

Suddenly all my senses were on alert. I heard someone coming up the stairs from the basement. *Oh no, they're coming up to bed!* I felt the panic surging up from deep in my belly into my throat. I held my breath so I could hear more clearly. I heard their footsteps going across the kitchen floor and the sound of someone opening the fridge door. Then came the whoosh of air escaping a bottle as the cap hit the countertop. And then again, another bottle opening; another cap. I let my breath escape from my lungs and sucked in another quick, deep breath.

This sounds promising.

As the footsteps descended the basement stairs, I heard laughter and someone whispering loudly, "Shh, you'll wake the girls." And then more laughter.

A wave of relief washed over me as I realized they would be staying up for quite some time. And with the relief came the security of knowing I had plenty of time to fall into a deep sleep long before the house became silent for the night.

And now, with the luxury of time on my side, I slowly glanced around my new room again, taking time to admire the walls, the dresser, the pictures. *My walls, my dresser, my pictures!* This was the first time in my life I had my very own room. Oh, I know. I slept in the rec room in our other house for a time, but everyone else got to use it during the day, too, so it wasn't really my very own room. And besides, that's where it happened. That's why I'm afraid of the dark now.

No, don't go there. Don't think about it. Think about something else. Anything else.

Now that it was only me and my younger sister living at home, we each got our own room. She had the larger room because it had to fit two twin beds in it. But my room had a double bed! For the first time in my life, I had my own double bed. And a big double dresser with a mirror on it. And a good size closet that I didn't have to share. I was now able to neatly spread out all my clothes in my closet and my drawers, with plenty of room to spare.

This room is going to be my sanctuary. The place I can go when I want to be alone. Alone to think, to plan, to write. Oh, I don't mind writing at the kitchen table, when I have privacy, that is. It's much more comfortable. But privacy is still an issue. Even though there are only four of us living here, and it really is such a big house compared to our last one, there still seems to be so little privacy.

That's because she's so nosy. She always wants to know what I'm writing. But it's private! It's all my deepest thoughts. All my secrets. She has no right to know what my thoughts are. They're mine. And if I want to share them, I will. But if I don't want to share them, I shouldn't be made to.

Okay, don't go there. You don't have to think bad things. Angry things. You can think whatever you want. Thinking is the one thing nobody else can control about you. They can make you do things you don't want to do and even say things you don't want to say. Well, sometimes. But they can't make you think something. You can lie. You can lead them to believe you think something that you don't really think. But inside, you know better. And that gives you your control. That's the real you. The one no one really knows.

Except William.

No, don't go there. You can't go there. It's too painful. Just think about something else. Anything else. Tomorrow. I'll think about tomorrow. But that makes me feel nervous. Stop. This is going to be good. This is what you wanted. A fresh start. A place where no one knows you. Where no one knows anything about you. Where you can tell your story in any way you want. They can see the you that you want them to see. They don't know what you've done.

And then I started to plan. To create. *Who is the person I want them to know? In a way, I am so many different people. I am the person the teachers know me to be. I am the person my girlfriends know me to be. I am the person that other adults know me to be. I am the person that boys know me to be. No, don't go there. Wait—why not? This is my chance. I get to be whoever I want to be. This is my fresh start.*

And then I started to feel excited again. About the day ahead of me and the life ahead of me. Things were going to be different from now on because this time I was going to do things differently.

As I lay there revelling in my enthusiasm, I suddenly realized I would never get to sleep unless I settled down and relaxed. So I took a slow, deep breath and then another. And as I began to relax into the rhythm of my breathing, I thought about William.

I thought about William being gone. The pain of the loss gripped me instantly. William had always been there for me. William was my rock. *And now I have no one. How can I possibly go on without William? No, don't go there.* But I couldn't help myself.

Then I thought about my mom's illness. *No, don't go there.* But William had been there when I was terrified. When I was gripped in fear and doubting my faith, William gave me the loving support and encouragement I needed to go on. William gave me hope when all I had was hopelessness.

Why did they have to leave?

And then I thought about when I'd been in the depths of despair. When I'd felt abandoned and unworthy of anyone's love. *No, don't go there.* But William was there. Loving me. I could feel the love right down to the core of my being.

And then I thought about that night. That night when it happened. And William was there. I would not be here now— breathing, thinking, planning, living—if it weren't for William. He saved my life.

But I don't have William anymore. William is gone. I'll never see William again. But I can always remember. I do remember. Even way back. How old was I then? I know I was young. I wasn't even in school yet.

Chapter 2

I was four years old. It was a beautiful, sunny day. My friend Noel and I were playing out in front of my house when I suddenly got an idea.

"Let's go out and look at the big street," I suggested.

"But we're not allowed," he answered.

I started to head toward the big street, with Noel reluctantly following.

"We'll only look at it," I said. *Surely that can't do any harm. Can it? Of course not! Besides, we're not little babies anymore. After all, I just turned four. I'm almost old enough for kindergarten.* And then I hesitated. *Mommy warned me many times not to go out to the big street. What could be out there that's so bad?* I started to feel nervous.

"Wait up," Noel called out as he shuffled to keep up.

"Come on. We're almost there." I was starting to feel excited as we got closer.

And there it was. The big street. *It sure is big!* I gulped as my eyes grew wide. *Wow.* There were so many cars. They were all going so fast. Not like on the street we lived on.

"Wow, it sure is big," Noel said, a look of wonder in his eyes.

"I'm scared," Noel said.

I didn't want Noel to know that I was scared too. "We'll be okay if we just stay on the sidewalk," I reassured him. I was trying so hard to be brave.

As we slowly started to move along the sidewalk, two grownups walked past us, so we stopped and just stood there watching. *Maybe we'll just follow behind them a little way. Then we'll go home.*

"Come on, Noel. Let's follow these grownups," I whispered as I started to follow them, with Noel shuffling behind.

"Where are we going?" he asked as he scurried to keep up.

"Just a little ways along," I said, not exactly sure myself.

After a little while, the adults stopped and faced the road and waited. So we stood back and waited, too. Then all the cars stopped and the people stepped onto the street and started to cross.

I wasn't sure what to do. I looked way back down the street from where we had come, and suddenly I didn't want to be here without the adults, so I stepped out onto the street to follow them.

"Come on, Noel. Hurry," I said as I started to run. Noel followed me across. Once we were on the other side, I looked back at the street and saw the cars start to move again. Then I looked for the adults. They were heading into the big store in front of us. We had been to that store before with my mommy. It had groceries and candies and so many amazing things.

"Let's go," I said, walking to the doors of the big store. We went inside and started to explore. *I found it—the aisle with the candies and chocolate bars and chips. Wow, there's so much to look at. Mm-mm.* I could almost taste them, just looking at them: the chocolate bars. And they were so big! Not like the little ones I'd had before. And so many. So, so many.

I would love to have some. There's so many. I looked around for Noel. He had wandered up the aisle to look at the chips and stuff. Then I looked back at the chocolate bars.

They wouldn't care if I took a few. I'm sure they wouldn't even notice them gone. As I started to think about taking some, I got nervous. I was afraid someone might know what I was thinking. I knew it was wrong to take some. But they looked so good. *As long as they don't see me taking them, they'll never know.* I picked a few from the shelf and held them. *I sure would like to have these.* I looked around and didn't see anyone. Even Noel was distracted, so he didn't see me shove them into my pants. Not my pockets. I shoved them down the front of my pants.

I started to walk quickly up the aisle and as I passed Noel I said, "Let's go," and I kept walking. I could feel my heart pounding and I just wanted to get as far away from the store as I could.

"Hey, kids," a man called out from behind me.

I froze. *Oh no, I've been caught! Should I run or should I turn to look at him?*

"Where's your parents?" he continued.

Noel started to speak and I cut him off. "They just went outside," I answered, and I grabbed Noel's arm and pulled at him to follow me. "We were just leaving to catch up to them."

We ran out to the street and over to the place where we had crossed earlier. I looked back at the store to see if the man was following us. Then I looked at the street. The cars were speeding by. They were going so fast. I wondered how we were going to get them to stop, the way they had before.

I began to panic. *How are we going to get back home!* I looked back at the store and my panic grew. *What if they discover the missing chocolate bars? What will I do then? I just want to go home.* I turned back to the street and saw that all the cars had stopped. Without a second thought, I started to run across the street.

"Let's go, Noel," I shouted.

When I got to the other side, I stopped and turned to see if Noel had made it across. Thump. He ran right into me. *Thank goodness!* In all my panic, I hadn't even looked to see if he was with me.

Once we were back on our side of the street, I began to feel safer. As we walked back toward our street, I pulled the chocolate bars out of my pants to show Noel.

"Look what I got," I said, trying to build up some excitement. But at that point, I didn't even want them anymore. I could still feel the lingering fright of the experience. I didn't like how I was feeling. *I wish I hadn't taken them.* I just wanted to be back home on our own street, where I felt safe.

By the time we arrived back to our street, we were both running. And when I could see my house in the distance, I let out a big breath. We had slowed down and were just strolling when I heard my mother calling me in for lunch. Suddenly, the panic and fear washed over me again. I shoved the chocolate bars into Noel's hands and said, "Hide these. Don't tell anyone you have them. I'll see you after lunch." And I ran home.

We were just finishing up lunch when the doorbell rang. I don't know why, but I suddenly felt this overwhelming sense of doom. I could feel my heart thumping in my throat. My father came into the kitchen with the chocolate bars in his hand, shouting, "Where did you get these? Don't lie to me—I already know!"

I didn't get a chance to respond. He was shouting, "You're a thief, and thieves have to be punished."

"You're going to get the belt," he yelled as he started to undo the belt buckle on his pants.

"No, Daddy, please," I pleaded. "I'll never do it again."

"You're damn right, you won't! I'll make sure of that, you little thief."

"Please, Daddy. Don't. I'm sorry," I begged.

"So you don't want the belt, eh? Then I'll have to call the police on you. And they'll come and take you to jail. Do you want that?"

"No, Daddy, please no!" I screamed.

"Make up your mind. It's either the belt or I call the police and have them take you away to jail. So which is it going to be?"

"Neither, Daddy, please. I'm sorry. I promise—I'll never do it again. Please, Daddy, please."

"You're going to be punished, one way or the other."

"No, Daddy, please. I've learned my lesson. I won't do it again."

"Will I decide, then?" He started to pull the belt out of the loops.

I was terrified. I wanted to run, but there was nowhere to go. There was no escaping it. I was going to get the belt or I was going to jail. Either choice was horrifying.

I panicked as I stood there watching him undo his belt. And then, as he got the last of the belt free from his pants, I screamed, "Call the police." I needed time to think. I thought if I stalled, I might come up with a third choice that wasn't so frightening.

But there was no time.

He immediately ran to the phone and picked it up and called the police. I was frozen in terror. I couldn't breathe. I felt my face burning with heat. *What's my daddy doing? He's supposed to love me and protect me. He doesn't love me. He's sending me to jail! I'll never see my sisters or brothers again. I'll never see my mommy again. My mommy! She's just standing there beside him, not saying a word. She's letting him do this. She isn't trying to stop him! She doesn't love me, either. I am bad. I am a bad, bad girl. My mommy and daddy don't love me. They want to send me away!*

I just stood there feeling defeated. My world was crumbling. I wasn't sure which was more horrifying—not being with my family ever again or going to jail. They both terrified me and I could see no way out. It was too late. He had already called the police. My daddy couldn't take it back. He had already told the police what I had done. They were coming for me.

I was frozen in terror. I felt light-headed.

"The police are on their way. So what do you think of that," he shouted.

I didn't respond. I was so terrified that I couldn't speak.

"Why you little thieving brat," he shouted, as he came toward me.

Suddenly I felt my father grab my arm and pull me toward my bedroom, yelling at me as he jerked me into the room. I felt the belt sear my skin. My back was on fire. And my arms and my legs. *What's happening? He already called the police and now he's giving me the belt, too!* He yelled as the belt came down on me, over and over. I couldn't hear what he was saying. All I could hear was my own screaming and the sound of his voice in the background.

Through the noise and the pain, I heard my mother shouting at my daddy. "That's enough John. She's had enough," I heard her say.

The pain was unbearable. But through the pain was this overwhelming confusion. I was screaming in pain as I tried to crawl up the bed to get away from the belt. Then came the anger. I understood my confusion. I suddenly realized that something wasn't right. I screamed through my pain as the belt came down over and over and over. "But you gave me a choice! You said for me to pick one and I did. And you called the police! You said I had a choice. You said pick one. It's not fair! I picked. It's not fair. It's not fair. Mommy, help me. Mommy, it's not fair. Please help me. Please."

And then it finally stopped. My mother was pulling my father off of me and then I heard the door slam. It was silent except for the crying I heard coming from myself. *How could this be? This isn't fair. It isn't fair. It isn't fair.*

I finally cried myself to sleep, where I found peace for a short while.

*

I woke up, feeling a sense of something different. Something had changed. Something important. I rolled over, and the sheets rubbed against my tender, welted skin. I began to feel the lingering pain on my body and I remembered.

I sat up on the side of my bed and thought over what had happened earlier. I felt numb. I wasn't sure if it was because I was still groggy from my sleep, or whether I had resigned myself to what was going to happen. Or maybe I just didn't really comprehend what was going to happen. No matter what, I knew that my life was over—at least the life I knew was over. I felt as though I was living inside a bad dream. It didn't feel real. Here I was, sitting on my bed, and that seemed normal enough. *So why can't my life just continue as if it was a bad dream and I finally woke up from it?*

I got up and walked out of my bedroom, still feeling emotionally drained and unsure of what I would face when I left my room. I walked down the hall and into the kitchen. My mommy was nursing my baby sister and my daddy was reading. *Seems pretty normal. How can everything be so different but yet seem so normal?*

My mommy looked up at me and casually said, "Why don't you get your sweater on and go outside to play."

The emotional numbness was gone! My heart started to pound and fear washed over me. "I can't go outside. The police will get me and take me away!" I screamed as panic took over.

"Just put your sister's sweater on. The police are looking for a little girl with a brown sweater. Your sister's sweater is red. They won't recognize you with the red sweater. Carolyn can wear your sweater."

I couldn't believe what she was suggesting! *The police will take my big sister Carol away instead of me. I can't let that happen. I'm the bad one! It wouldn't be fair if they took her away because of me. That just isn't right. How can my mom not see that? How can she let them take my sister away?*

"But the police will take Carol away if she has my sweater on," I argued.

"Don't be silly. Carol doesn't look anything like you. She has dark brown hair and yours is red."

"But you said they're looking for a little girl with a brown sweater.

"Yes that's right, a little girl with red hair and a brown sweater. She'll be okay and so will you," she reassured.

It still didn't feel right. It did make sense that neither one of us would look like the description, but I was still afraid to go outside.

I guess my mother could sense my fear so she suggested, "Why don't you just go out to the backyard to play. They won't see you out there."

That makes sense. They'll never see me in the backyard. I can do that. But I still didn't feel all that excited about going outside to play—period. *I wish this day could be over. I want to be happy again. I want to be happy playing.*

My mother had put the baby back in her crib and was putting Carol's sweater on me. As she did up the last button, panic suddenly gripped me again. "I have to go to the bathroom," I blurted out, and I ran out of the kitchen and down the hall. I really needed to talk to my secret friends. I ran down the hall and into the bathroom. I closed and locked the door. Then I turned and leaned against the door.

Just breathe. Deep breaths. Slow, deep breaths. As I started to breathe, I could feel the panic slowly easing. I opened my eyes and walked over to the toilet. I put the lid down and sat. I took another deep breath. I stared at the tiles on the wall.

William, I called out in my mind. *William, are you here?*

I picked one of the tiles on the wall and stared at it. I took slow, even breaths and stared. I started to feel my body relax and I just kept staring at the one tile on the wall. I was no longer aware of anything around me. Just that one tile.

Hello, luv, I heard in my mind. The voice appeared to be coming from somewhere off to my left.

William. You're here!

And how are you, dear child, on this lovely day?

Not so good.

I'm not quite sure when William first came to me, but I have come to cherish our talks together. William had explained to me that they are a group of invisible friends who came to me to help me. To teach me. I didn't fully understand why they were all called William. They said they would explain it to me in greater detail when I was better able to understand. From what I could sense, a smaller group of them was represented in the tiles. Sort of like each tile was a little house with a family in it. And all of the tiles together were like their own little town, and William was the spokesperson. When they first said that to me, I didn't know what it meant. They explained that a *spokesperson* is someone who talks for a group of people. That made sense to me, so they left it at that. They said they would try to always talk to me at a level I could comprehend, but as teachers, they would also give me the chance to grow and learn. They also taught me that *comprehend* is another word that means *understand*. They've taught me a lot of words and their meanings. My mommy uses a lot of big words that I don't always understand. Sometimes when I ask her what they mean, she doesn't always explain it in a way that helps me to know the meaning. So the next time I talk with William, they teach me what the words mean. I am usually able to understand better when they show me what the words mean.

Sometimes William talks to me with words; other times they talk to me with pictures. But it's always in my mind that we talk. I don't exactly remember when they first came to visit me, but they've been with me for a long time now, and I really treasure my time with them.

It is such a lovely day today. You should be feeling wonderful.

I was bad today. I looked down to the floor.

That's not possible, little one. You are a precious soul. It is not possible that you are bad.

My daddy says I'm bad.

Your father is mistaken, little one.

But I stole something and I lied about it. I felt the tears well up in my eyes.

You also made a mistake, dear child. That does not make you a bad person. You needed to have that experience in order to grow.

I don't understand.

How did you feel, just before you took the chocolate bars?

How did you know they were chocolate bars? I asked, my eyes widening.

We've told you before. We are always with you. We know everything about you, little one.

But then why didn't I know you were there? Why didn't I feel that you were with me?

You did, dear child.

I did? What do you mean?

We ask again. How did you feel just before you took the chocolate bars?

I thought for a moment. *I felt scared.*

And did that feel good or bad to you?

Bad. Of course it felt bad.

That was us. We were warning you that you shouldn't do something when you don't feel good about it.

Why didn't you just tell me not to do it?

It doesn't work that way, little one. You need to pay closer attention to how you feel. When something you are thinking about doing feels bad, you would be better off not doing it. Do you understand?

I think so.

And are you feeling better, dear child?

A little. And then I remembered! *My daddy hates me. And he punished me twice! He told me I could pick my punishment and I did. But then he gave me both. That wasn't fair. He did it because he hates me. He says I am a bad girl.*

Your father was afraid. That is why he behaved that way.

Afraid? What do you mean?

Your father was afraid for you. He thinks that it is his job to teach you right from wrong. He decided that what you did was wrong and that he needed to teach you it was wrong by punishing you. But he was mistaken.

But I did do something wrong. You said so. You tried to warn me not to do it.

It was only wrong because you didn't feel good when you did it. Do you understand the difference?

I think so. But why did he punish me twice? That wasn't fair.

It happened because you believed him when he said you were bad. And he acted out of misguided fear. It's important for you to know that you are a perfect little girl. We love you and we know that you are wonderful.

A warmth washed over me. I could feel their love for me and it made me feel better. I thought about how much I love them and how thankful I was that they were my friends.

You feel so much better now. We are pleased.

I love you, William. Thank you so much.
Our love for you is greater than you know.

I sensed that our meeting was over for now. As I got up from the toilet seat, feeling the wonderful glow of their love, I tried to remember when it was that they had first come to me.

I left the bathroom and went outside in the yard to play. I picked up a ball from the ground and started to throw it up in the air. It bounced down on the patio and back up. I caught it and threw it up in the air again. And then it came to me. I remembered the time when I first discovered William.

*

I was only two years old. No, maybe more like two-and-a-half. I remembered my mother carrying me out to the backyard, saying, "Now you stay in here and play with your toys while your sister finishes her nap."

What does she mean, stay in here? I looked through the link fence that separated the backyard from the driveway. *How am I supposed to get out? Oh well, it doesn't matter.* I turned around to see what I had to play with. *A ball. That looks like fun!* I ran over to pick up the big, bright orange ball. "Weeeeee," I squealed as I threw the ball up in the air and watched it fall to the ground and bounce back up by itself. *This is fun. Lots of fun. I love this.*

"Hehehehe. Ouch!" The ball hit me in the face. *I better change the way I throw this up in the air.* I threw it out in front of me. It banged against the fence and bounced back toward me. *Oh, this is good.* I did it again. And again. This was fun.

"Oh, oh." The ball had gone over the fence. I ran over to see where it had gone. It was rolling down the driveway. Then it stopped part way down and over to the side, in the bushes. I started to cry.

"My ball. Mama, ball." Nothing. My mama didn't come. *I want my ball.* I started to climb the fence. *This isn't so hard. I'm almost at the top.* I looked over the top and down the other side. It was really far! And scary. I looked back to the ground behind me. It was just as far and just as scary. Then I looked forward to where my ball was. *There it is. I want my ball.*

I swung my leg over the top of the fence, then the other one. "Oh-oh."

I lost my footing and was dangling from the fence. *Now what do I do? Oh, there it is.* My foot found the fence and I climbed the rest of the way down. I turned around to see if my ball was still there. *Yes, there it is.* It hadn't moved. I ran over to it and reached down to grab it.

"Whoa." Thump. I landed on my bum. *That didn't hurt at all.*

"Hmmm?" *What's that squirmy thing in the dirt? Maybe it tastes good. Let's see.* I reached out for it. *Where'd it go? It was right there? Humph, oh well. There's my ball.* I reached out and grabbed my ball. I hugged it. *Mmm, it smells good.* I licked it. *Not bad. Not great, but not bad.* I tried to stand up while hugging my ball, but it just wasn't working. I didn't want to let go of my ball though. I lay over top of my ball and managed to walk my feet up closer to the ball, my bum stuck up in the air. *There we go.* I used the ball to brace myself and with a final shove, I stood up, the ball still in my arms.

"Whoa." I almost fell again. The ball dropped out of my arms and bounced a few times, rolling down to the bottom of the driveway. Off I ran, down the driveway to get my ball.

I was just reaching down to grab my ball, when I heard giggling and squealing coming from across the street. I looked up and across to where the noise was coming from. I could see a little baby in a playpen. *That looks like fun.* I ran out in the street toward the little baby.

I reached the bottom of the other driveway when the noise stopped. The baby was standing in the playpen watching me. Then the giggling and squealing started again. I ran up the driveway and stood in front of the playpen. We both stared at each other for a while and then the baby giggled again.

I liked the sound of his giggle. He was so pretty. We both moved up to the bars on the playpen and I kissed him. He smelled so good. He looked so good. *What a pretty baby.*

"I love you." *I want to hug you.* I reached through the bars and hugged him. *Pretty baby.* I kissed him again on the cheek. *I love you. I love you, I love you,* I thought as I squeezed him and kissed him, and bit into his cheek!

Suddenly, the baby let out a screech. There was a long wailing sound and he started to gasp for air in between. Something was wrong with the baby, but I didn't understand what.

Then this lady came running out of the house and ran to the baby. She picked him up and started to sooth him.

Oh that's good. This lady will make the baby all better. And then I heard the lady gasp.

"What have you done to him?" she yelled as she looked down at me. All of a sudden she grabbed my arm and started to drag me down the driveway. I couldn't keep up with her, she was walking so fast.

Yank, yank, yank. My arm was being stretched. It felt like she was going to rip it right off. Then I felt the searing pain as my legs scraped the driveway. I couldn't seem to keep my feet on the ground, she was moving so fast.

I could barely think through the pain, the yelling, the baby crying and me crying too. *What's happening?*

"What'd I do? What'd I do?" *Did I say it out loud or did I just think it?* I wasn't sure.

We were at the front door to my house and my mama came running to the door. Now my mama and the lady were yelling at each other. It was so loud and they were shouting so fast. I couldn't make out what they were saying, but they sure were mad. It was scary. They both sounded so angry.

My mama will protect me from that mean lady. Even though I couldn't make out the words they were shouting, I could sense that the anger was directed at me. *But why? What did I do?*

My mama grabbed me by the arm and pulled me up into the house. She was still yelling at me as she pulled me down the hallway.

"Do you want me to bite you?" she threatened. "Do you? Do you?"

I could tell that this wouldn't be a good thing. She was so angry and I didn't understand why. *What's happening?* I thought. *I don't understand. What did I do? Why is everyone so mad?*

And then I felt the searing pain as my mama bit down on my arm. I couldn't breathe. *Oh please, make the pain stop. Stop, stop, please.* And the worst of it did. My mother had stopped biting me.

I could still feel the throbbing as I looked down at the bite mark on my arm. I was so confused. *I don't remember ever feeling any pain with biting before.* I lay there on the floor, whimpering as the throbbing subsided and left me with a sharp stinging where mama had bit me.

I could hear my mama talking in the background. She wasn't yelling anymore, but she sounded sad. "It's my fault," I heard her say. "When we play, I nibble at her. She doesn't understand how to control herself. She didn't realize she was hurting the baby. It was just her way of showing love and affection. I better not play that way with her anymore."

I hurt the baby! That's what I heard her say. But how? The bite. When mama bit me just now, it really, really hurt. Oh no! I hurt the baby when I was loving him.

I knew there was something very important in all this. I wasn't sure I fully understood, but, somehow, playing, loving and biting were all mixed up together and they shouldn't be. I got up from the floor and wandered into my bedroom. I was still feeling bad about what I'd done to the little baby. And confused.

As I reached for my dolly, I suddenly realized that I had to go pee-pee. *Oh no. Hold it, hold it,* I was thinking as I ran to the bathroom. I slammed the bathroom door behind me and ran to the toilet. I pulled the diaper down to my ankles. *Hold it, hold it. Almost there.* I pulled myself up onto the toilet. *Aah aah.*

As I sat there on the toilet, feeling the relief, I thought I heard something.

Top of the morning to you, little one.

I frowned in confusion.

And how are you doing on this fine morning, dear child?

I looked around the bathroom. I couldn't see anything. Everything looked normal.

We're here, little one. Close your eyes and we'll show you.

I closed my eyes. In my mind I could see the squares on the bathroom wall. And in each square, I pictured a family of little people. And all the squares together felt like one big family.

"Who are you?" I whispered out loud.

You don't need to speak with your voice. Just speak with your thoughts. We can hear your thoughts.

Who are you? I thought in my mind.

That's it. You've got it right. What a fast learner you are, little one.

But who are you? I couldn't see anything when I opened my eyes. I could see them only when my eyes were closed.

We're your friends. Your teachers. We're here to help you.

What does teachers *mean?*

Teachers *are people who know more than you do, who help you to learn and know what they know. Do you understand?*

I think so. Like Mommy and Daddy, right? And like my big brothers, Teddy and Kevin, right?

Close enough for now.

My name's Joanne. What's yours?

You can call us whatever you choose. What would you like to call us?

I don't know.

Close your eyes and it will come to you.

I closed my eyes. *But there's so many of you.*

Just pick one name.

As I sat there with my eyes closed, a name came into my head. *William. Your name is William. Right?*

William is a fine name. You can call us William.

I felt so pleased with myself that I was able to figure out their name without them telling me. *How come you only have one name, but there are so many of you?*

Just think of one of us as the spokesperson for all of us, okay?

What's a spokesperson?

A spokesperson *is someone who speaks on behalf of a group of people.*

What does behalf *mean?*

Behalf *means for. So when we say to think of us as one person who is speaking* on behalf of *all of us, we mean that we are all thinking the same, so the spokesperson is speaking for all of us. Does that help?*

Yes, I think so.

So, let's start this again. How are you feeling on this fine day, dear child?

And then I remembered. I remembered hurting the baby and Mommy biting me and hurting me. I didn't feel as bad about Mommy hurting me anymore. My arm hurt only a little bit now. But I still felt really bad about hurting the little baby.

I feel bad. I hurt a little baby today. But I didn't mean to. I love the baby. How come I hurt the baby without meaning to? I don't understand.

Dear little one. We know you didn't mean to harm the baby. You needed to do this so you could learn and grow. You are just a little baby yourself. Do not worry about this. The baby is fine.

But, I'm not a little baby. I'm a big girl now. Look it, I even use the big potty now!

We can see that. You have grown a great deal.

I beamed with pride.

Do you understand that you have done nothing wrong? You didn't mean to hurt anyone. We could feel the love you feel for the baby and we are very proud of you.

You are? And then I felt this warm rush of love inside of me. I could feel William sending me this love and it felt so wonderful. I suddenly felt a love for William, as well. I could feel myself sending my love back as I felt them sending their love to me. The warmth and comfort I felt was so strong. My heart sang with joy!

I love you, William!

Dear, dear child. We love you, too. Our love for you is greater than you know.

I felt the meeting was over, so I jumped down from the toilet, pulled up my diaper and ran out of the bathroom, still feeling the joy and excitement of our time together.

Chapter 3

I turned six the summer my parents broke up. I didn't really understand what that meant. My father was away a lot on business, so I didn't automatically connect the break-up with not seeing him. What it did mean to me was that I would be living in a different house and going to a different school. And even more immediately, for the first several weeks of the new school year, I would be going to a temporary school.

We had been staying at a farm near our cottage for the summer, while my parents organized their break-up and got our house packed up. During that summer, we saw our mother only when she came up on weekends with my baby sister. My two older brothers, my older sister and I got to stay at the neighbour's farm during the week, and we would go back to the cottage on weekends.

It was a wonderful time for me. The dad was a very kind, quiet man and the mom was a large, strong, jolly person. I felt happy and safe with them. And food—there were always delicious, different foods to eat. We got to drink milk that had come right from the cow, and they made their own butter. They made the most amazing homemade chicken soup and they even put Worcestershire sauce in it! I know it sounds awful, but it was so good.

There were lots of kids in the neighbour's family to play with and so many new things to explore. There were cows and chickens and dogs and cats. And there was this huge barn where they stored the hay. That was my favourite place of all. It was like having our own huge playhouse. There was a big loft that we got up to by climbing up a tall ladder. The older kids, including my brothers, had to do chores for some of the day, but us younger kids were allowed to just play, play, play.

When the summer came to an end and it was time to go back to school, our new house wasn't ready for us to move into. My mother explained that the previous owners wouldn't be moving out until the end of September, so we would be going to the local, rural school near our cottage for a few weeks. She explained that it was a small school and that there would be two grades in each classroom. I was going into Grade one, so that meant that there would also be a Grade two class in the same room. I wasn't sure about all this. After all, I was just getting used to the whole school thing, and now she was telling me that I would be going to a different school.

"But what about all my friends?" I asked. "I won't know anybody."

"Of course you will. Your brothers and sister will be there too," she said.

"But they won't be in my class," I argued.

"Your sister will be," she explained. "Carol is going into Grade two, so she will be in the same class as you. You get to be in with the older kids. Won't that be fun?"

I did like the sound of that.

Finally, the first day of school arrived. My mother was driving us there and it seemed to be taking forever. It was so far away. She talked and talked while she drove. It was as if she was trying to convince us of something. She seemed nervous. An uneasy feeling started to wash over me. It felt like something bad was going to happen. She was saying words of encouragement, but, somehow, something just didn't feel right. *What is it? Is she trying to trick us? I'm glad my big brothers and my sister are with me.* I didn't like the way I was feeling. *Are we ever going to get there?*

I could hear my mother saying that the school bus would be picking us up after school and that, after today, we would be taking the bus to school and back. "Won't that be exciting?"

"School bus, what's a school bus?" I asked. I had never heard of a school bus before.

You're supposed to walk to school, aren't you? Doesn't everybody walk to school? But it seems to be taking so long to get there. How far are we going? How far away is this school, anyway?

I could hear my mom talking about school buses in the background, but I wasn't really listening. I was lost in my own thoughts, getting more and more nervous. No, I was getting scared. Something felt "off." I couldn't quite put my finger on it, but I didn't like it.

"We're here," my mother chimed as we pulled into the parking area of a small, brick building.

This can't be the school. I gazed at the building. It seemed so small for a school. It looked more like an oversized house. As it turned out, there were only three classrooms in the whole school: one for Grades one and two together, one for three and four together and one for five and six.

The morning went very slowly. The lessons weren't difficult, but we had to sit in a seat attached to a desk for a long, long time. That was hard. We didn't get to play in class like we had last year. *And where are all the toys? Maybe it's just this school?*

A loud bell rang. Finally, it was lunchtime. I was so hungry and I couldn't wait to get out and play. We had handed our lunch bags to the teacher when we first arrived in the morning and she was now calling out each of our names to come and get the bag with our name on it.

I gobbled up my sandwich and then my apple. I wanted to finish my lunch as fast as possible so I could go out and play. When I got to the two cookies in my bag, I was torn. I really wanted to go out and play, but I loved cookies and I wanted them to last as long as possible. I started to eat a little slower. *Mmm, these sure are good.* It still didn't take long for me to eat them. After all, there were only two of them.

Once I was finished, I packed my apple core and sandwich wrapper into the paper lunch bag and scrunched it up. I got up from my seat to throw it in the wastebasket when the teacher bellowed, "Sit down right now!"

I quickly looked around the room to see who she was yelling at. *Was it me? It had to be.* Everyone else was still seated at their desks, eating. *What'd I do wrong? How come she's yelling at me?*

I quickly explained, "But I'm just throwing my garbage away." *Uh-oh. That wasn't the right thing to say.*

Suddenly, she was grabbing my arm and shoving me back into my seat. I was so confused.

"Nobody gets out of their seat until I say so," she shouted out to the whole class.

So that was it. How was I supposed to know? She should have told us before. Instead, I get in trouble and I didn't even know. I don't like her. And I don't like this school. I sat at my desk for what seemed like forever. I had eaten my lunch so quickly that now I had to wait for everyone else to finish theirs. She had told us in the morning that we would be able to go out and play after we finished eating our lunch. *I guess that meant that everyone had to finish first.*

Finally, everyone was finished and she told us we could get up and throw out our garbage. She told us to line up in front of the door and she would lead us out into the school yard. Once we were out in the yard, it was fun. A bunch of my classmates came up and asked to play with me. Even the older ones wanted to play with me! They thought it was funny when I got up in class and made the teacher yell at me. We joked around and played, and I felt good again.

When we were all seated in our class after lunch, the teacher told the Grade ones that we had to lay our heads down on our desks and have a nap, while she taught a lesson to the Grade twos.

Have a nap? Is she crazy? I'm not a little baby! I haven't had to nap in a long time. I'm not sleepy. How can I have a nap when I'm not sleepy?

"Heads down now," she shouted. "Eyes closed. And I don't want to hear a peep out of any of you."

I put my head down and closed my eyes. I felt restless and uncomfortable. I was wide awake and this was boring. I wasn't happy. I didn't like this at all. I sat there with my head down, listening to her talk to the Grade twos.

"Okay, class. Who can tell me a word that starts with the letter 'A'?" she asked.

Silence.

"Come on now. Someone must be able to give me a word that starts with 'A'?"

Silence.

"Cathy, what about you?"

Nothing.

"Come on, Cathy, give me a word that starts with 'A'."

"I don't know, teacher," Cathy said quietly.

She doesn't know! That's impossible. How could she not know? It's so easy. Apple. *Say* apple*! Or* animal. *Say* animal. *Or* alphabet *or* alligator. *This is so easy. I'm only in Grade one and I know. How come the Grade twos don't know? They must know. It's too easy.*

"Okay, class, someone must know. Tommy?"

Silence.

"Mark?"

Nothing.

They really don't know! I can't believe it! Maybe I should help them?

"Apple," I whispered.

Silence.

"Apple," I whispered a little louder.

"That's right—apple. Who said that?" the teacher asked. The class was quiet. No one said anything. "Come, now, don't be shy. Apple is right," she urged. "Can anyone give me another word that starts with 'A'?"

Nothing. I couldn't believe it! "Animal," I whispered.

The class started to giggle. And I giggled.

"Who said that?" the teacher demanded.

I could hear whispering and giggling.

Bang! The teacher's ruler came crashing down on my desk. I looked up, my heart pounding. The teacher was staring down at me with a scary look on her face. She was furious.

"I told you to keep your head down and keep quiet," she bellowed. "Don't you speak up again. I mean it. You keep quiet and keep your head down. I won't tell you again."

"But I was just trying to help," I said.

She banged the ruler down on my desk so hard my whole body jerked.

She was so mad. I couldn't believe it. I was just helping. *What's the big deal? No one knew the answer, but I did. Why can't I give my answer?* But I didn't say anything. I just put my head down. I could still hear whispering and giggling from the rest of the class.

"All right, that's enough. Settle down. Now can someone tell me a word that starts with the letter 'B'?"

Silence. I was amazed. *Why didn't these older kids know the answer?* It seemed so easy to me. *B . . . baby, B . . . ball, basket, balloon. How can they not know?* I wanted to show the class how smart I was, but I didn't want to get in trouble again. *Maybe if I whisper really quiet, the teacher won't hear me.* "Baby," I whispered as quietly as I could. Nothing. I thought for sure that the boy right beside me would be able to hear me. "Ball," I whispered, just a little louder.

"Ball," the boy beside me shouted out.

"That's right, Jimmy. Very good. Now can you give me another word that begins with 'B'?"

But Jimmy didn't say anything.

"Come on Jimmy, give me another word," the teacher encouraged.

"Umm. I don't know," he said quietly.

"Balloon," I whispered.

"Balloon," Jimmy quickly said, as the class began to giggle.

Suddenly, the teacher grabbed my arm and yanked me out of my chair. She yelled as she jerked me and dragged me to the front of the class. She said I was a bad little girl. "You think you're so smart? Well I'll show you what happens to bad little girls who don't do as they're told," she bellowed. Then she grabbed my hand and twisted it around as she smashed the ruler down into my palm.

Just as the ruler was about to come down onto my hand again, I pulled it back and shouted, "No!"

The ruler hit my teacher's hand! Her face turned deep red with anger. She grabbed me and lifted me up off my feet and carried me to her chair. Then she sat down with me draped over her lap, holding me tightly so I couldn't move. "How dare you," she shouted as she hit me on my bum with the ruler, over and over.

I felt the pain sear through my underpants and onto my skin. I screamed and pleaded with her to stop as I wiggled and kicked my legs, trying to break free of her grip. Finally, it stopped. She lifted me off her lap and stood me up. I was crying as she shoved me in the direction of my desk.

"Now go sit down and I don't want to hear another word out of you," she warned.

I slowly walked back to my desk. I could feel the sting of the ruler as I sat down. I heard the whispering of the class, but I couldn't make out what they were saying. I didn't care. I felt like I was in a fog. In fact, I felt that way for quite a while. It wasn't until afternoon recess until I started to feel a little better.

Shortly after arriving home at the end of the day, my older brother Kevin came into the room I was playing in and started to tease me about getting the strap at school.

"How do you know?" I asked.

"Carol told me and she told Mom, too. You're in big trouble. Mom's looking for you. You're going to get it. She's really mad!"

I could feel a lump forming in my throat and my face burning up. I was gripped in fear of what my mom would do. And Carol. *How could she? She knows we're not supposed to tattle on each other. How could she tell Mom on me?* Fear turned to anger as I thought about my sister telling on me. And then anger turned to fear when I heard my mother calling to me.

"Joanne, get in the kitchen right now," she screamed.

I slowly made my way into the kitchen, trying to figure out what I should say. *How can I get out of this?*

"I heard you got the strap at school today. Is that true?" she accused.

"No," I blurted out.

"Don't lie to me. How could you do this? I have too much on my mind right now. I don't need this," she yelled, getting louder and louder. Madder and madder.

Suddenly, she grabbed the belt and started toward me.

And I ran.

She screamed as she chased me around the large kitchen table, swinging the belt when she thought she was close enough to make contact. She was getting madder and madder. And I was getting more and more frightened as she threatened that it would be a lot worse when she caught me, if I didn't stop running. I didn't know what to do. I kept running around the table and she kept running after me, yelling and threatening. Her threats were getting more and more terrifying.

I panicked. *I can't keep running forever. And if she catches up to me, it'll be worse.*

I stopped dead in my tracks and pleaded, "Don't, Mom, please. I was already punished. It's not fair. The teacher already punished me at school."

The belt came crashing down on me as I dropped to the ground and curled up in a ball, trying to protect myself.

"Please, Mom, no more. I've had enough. I learned my lesson. I won't do it again," I promised.

"Don't you dare cause me any more trouble with this school. Do you hear me?"

"Yes, Mom. I won't. I promise."

"Now go to your room until you're called down for supper."

But I couldn't let it go. "How come Carol isn't in trouble for tattling?" I pushed.

"Just get to your room," she answered.

So I did. But I still didn't understand. *First, I get in trouble at school, when all I was doing was trying to help out the stupid Grade twos. I got the strap and that wasn't fair. Then, I get home and I get punished again. Mom didn't even want to know what I did to get the strap. She didn't care. That wasn't fair. And then, Carol tattles on me and she doesn't even get in trouble for it. Mom is always telling us we have to stick up for each other. That we're not allowed to tattle on each other. I don't like my new school and I don't like Carol anymore. I don't trust her. From now on, I'll have to be careful about what I say and do around her.*

This is all so confusing. I want to live in my real home. I want to go to my old school. I hate my teacher and I hate this school. I don't want to move to our new house. I want my old life back. I lay there on my bed for the longest time, just thinking. I felt frightened when I thought about this new, uncertain life ahead of me. And then I thought, *William! I haven't talked to William all summer! Oh no. What if they didn't leave my old house? What if I couldn't talk to them anymore?*

I jumped up from my bed and went running into the bathroom.

I looked around the bathroom. There were no tiles on the wall! I started to panic.

Wait. Just calm down. Take deep breaths. William would never abandon me. They love me. And I love them. They would know that I moved. They would follow me. Wouldn't they?

I sat on the lid of the toilet and closed my eyes. I took a few deep breaths and started to relax.

William, William. William? Are you here? I felt my heart skip a beat. I could feel a lump forming in my throat. I swallowed. *Just keep breathing deeply. Just breathe. Don't think of anything but breathing, just like William taught me.*

Hello, luv! And how are you on this wonderful day?

My heart soared! *William. You're here!*

Of course we're here. Where else would we be, dear child?

I was afraid you wouldn't know where to find me.

We are wherever you are. We thought you understood that.

I sorta did. I just wasn't sure. I got scared. But I did my breathing, just like you told me to. And here you are.

Yes. And here we are, little one. You have learned well. We are very pleased with you.

You are? But what about today? I didn't have a very good day. I had to go to this awful school. And my teacher is mean. She spanked me! For nothing. And then my mom gave me the belt too! How come I'm always getting into trouble? I don't mean to do bad things. Why am I always doing bad things? I must be a bad person. I'm a bad person, aren't I?

Dear child. You are not a bad person. We think you are perfect, just the way you are.

But why am I always getting into trouble, then?

You needed to have this experience in order to learn and grow, dear one.

You always say that!

It is the truth.

But how come all my learning and growing has to feel so bad?

It doesn't, dear one.

But then, how come it does feel so bad all the time?

Did you feel bad all day long today?

I thought about this for a minute. *Well, no. The whole day didn't feel bad. Just the parts where I got in trouble and got spanked and got the belt.*

So tell us, what parts of the day felt good?

I thought again. *I liked feeling smart. I liked knowing the answers the Grade twos didn't know. I liked being popular with the new kids. And I liked playing in the schoolyard at recess and lunchtime. And I liked taking the school bus home from school.*

Anything else?

Oh, and most of all, I love that you followed me from my old house! I love talking to you right now.

And we love talking with you as well, dear one.

I've missed you. Why didn't you come to see me all summer?

We are always with you, dear child.

But how come you didn't speak to me?

You were having so much fun, you just didn't notice us there. We were having fun, right along with you. When you were laughing and singing and playing and appreciating your life, we were laughing and singing and appreciating every moment with you. And most of all, we were appreciating you, sweet one!

And there it was. That familiar warmth filling me up with their love. My heart sang with the joy of their presence. And my heart sent out so much love and appreciation to them. I felt so fortunate, so blessed, to have them in my life.

I must be a good person! Otherwise, you wouldn't love me so much, right?

Can you feel it? Can you feel our hearts singing in joy at your realization?

Yes! I feel it! I feel you! I feel your love and it makes me feel excited. I love you so much, William. Thank you.

Our love for you is greater than you know.

I could tell that it was time to leave. To get on with my life until the next time. And it felt so wonderful to know there would be a next time!

I got up and left the bathroom, humming a familiar tune, as I walked back to my room.

Chapter 4

I lay there in my bed, staring at the ceiling in my new room and thinking about the last few months. It was hard to believe I'd turned six just over two months ago, and I was already going to be going to my third school since the school year had started. We'd spent a wonderful summer alternating between our cottage, which I loved, and our neighbour's farm, and we'd just moved into our new home without my father.

I thought about the school we'd had to go to near our cottage for the first few weeks of the school year. None of the school kids lived anywhere near us, so I couldn't play with them after school. And Mommy said I wouldn't be seeing any of my friends that I grew up with ever again! She said I would make new friends when we got settled into our new home. I did have my two older brothers and my older sister to play with, but I could play with them any time. I wanted to play with my own friends.

Our new house seemed smaller than our old one, even though there was a whole second storey that we didn't have before. There were lots and lots of houses on our street. A lot more than on our other street, where I used to live. And our front and back yards were a lot smaller. But Mommy told us there were loads and loads of kids in the neighbourhood and they all went to the same school we were going to go to.

        *

When the day finally arrived to go to our new school, I was excited. I was a little concerned that it would be like that other temporary school, but mostly, I was excited. *After all, there couldn't be that many mean teachers around, could there?* And Mommy had said the new school was even bigger than the first school I'd gone to, and I loved that school.

After breakfast that day, we all piled into our car, except for my baby sister Shirley. Someone was looking after her while we all went to school and Mommy went to her new job. We were all excited, trying to talk over each other to be heard. That was a pretty regular occurrence in a family with five kids ranging from two years old to ten. My mommy finally shouted out to us to be quiet.

"You need to pay attention to where we're going, so you'll know the way back home. I can't drive you after this morning, so look around and remember the route we're taking. This is the way you'll walk to and from school from now on. I'll be home to give you your lunch every day this week, but after that I won't always be able to come home at lunchtime," she explained as she pulled the car out of the driveway.

We all sat quietly, gazing out the car windows, buried in our own thoughts, as Mommy pointed out things for us to remember so we could find our way back home at lunchtime.

"See, now there's the shopping plaza with the grocery store, pharmacy and variety store. Remember, we went there yesterday? That's where you'll turn in to get to our street. Everyone remembers our new address, right?"

We all jumped in, rhyming off our address. I was being very serious about saying it precisely, but my brothers were making a joke about it. Kevin was going to be nine in a couple of weeks and Teddy was already ten.

"Mom, we got it. This is easy. We know how to get home, so don't worry," Kevin said.

"Yes, but what about your sisters? Are you going to walk them home at lunch today?" she argued.

"No, Ma. No way. Aw, we don't have to, do we Mom? Okay, okay, we'll be quiet."

"Now see this street to the right, at the lights coming up? That's where Mommy's working now. Down that street, in the office of a factory."

"What's a factory?" I asked.

"They make paint there, but we can talk about that later. You need to pay attention. Now if you look straight ahead, you'll see a crosswalk. See those big Xs hanging over the road? That means it's a crosswalk, where you can walk across the street. See the man with the stop sign and the bright orange vest? He will help you across the street. You are not allowed to cross until he says so. Do you understand?"

"Yes, Mommy," I said.

"Now, see how we've had to stop, and he's holding up the stop sign and walking into the middle of the road? See how the kids are able to cross the road with him? Now, if you look up ahead, there's a cemetery on the left side of the street and another street on the right. Also, look, there's another plaza there to the right, at the street. That's where we're going to turn. And this is the street where your new school is."

As we turned the corner, my mommy continued, "See, there's your new school. Look how big it is! And look at all the kids! You're going to love it here."

I was barely paying attention at that point. The school really was big. I could feel the excitement welling up inside me. There were loads and loads of kids coming from all directions, heading around to the back of the school. As we pulled into the large parking lot, I could see the back area of the school. It was huge! There was a large paved area, where a whole bunch of kids were playing, and this huge, huge field with grass and baseball diamonds, where more kids were playing. It was amazing!

We all got out of the car, and Mommy took us into the school. I was starting to get nervous again. Everything was so unfamiliar. And so big. We walked down a hall, around a corner, around another corner and into an office. *How am I ever going to remember how to get around in here? I've already forgotten how we got here, from outside.* A nice lady was talking to Mommy when the bell rang. And rang and rang. When it stopped, I heard the lady saying that we would wait until all the kids were in their classrooms and then she would take us to each of our new classes.

Mommy spoke up, saying, "Okay kids, I'm going to leave now because I have to get to work. I want you to behave yourselves. I'll see you at lunch."

I suddenly felt so small. And a little scared. I felt my face growing warm and a small lump forming in my throat. I was really glad my brothers and sister were with me. I couldn't quite be sure whether I was more scared or more excited. It felt strange—I was both.

When the lady took me to my new classroom, my sister was still with me. My brothers had been dropped off, one at a time, as we walked down this long, long hallway. The lady had knocked at the classroom door, the same way she had for each of my brothers. The door opened and there stood this beautiful lady, with a bright, warm smile showering down on me.

"Hello, Joanne. It's so nice to meet you. Why don't we go into the classroom and introduce you to the rest of your classmates. How does that sound?"

I was spellbound. Her voice sounded like a singing bird. She was wonderful. *I'm going to love it here!*

The morning went so fast, I couldn't believe it was lunchtime already. The bell rang and we all exited in an orderly fashion. Once outside, everyone started to play and goof around. Some kids just strolled along, others ran and others pushed and shoved, laughing and playing an unofficial form of tag. I found myself just moving along with the crowd. Everyone seemed to be moving in the same direction, so I followed. There were so many kids. It was fun watching the older kids laughing and goofing around as we walked. And I kept walking. Slowly, kids started to break off and head in different directions.

"See you after lunch," I heard over and over as kids broke off from the crowd and ran toward their separate destinations.

I hadn't spotted my brothers or sister, so I latched on to a small group of older kids and followed them. I figured they would know best how I could find my way home.

The crowd grew thinner and thinner, until, finally, the last of the kids I was following had run up their driveway and into their home. I continued to walk a short distance, when I remembered the crosswalk! I hadn't passed the crosswalk yet. I stopped. I looked around. Nothing looked familiar. The houses didn't look the same as the ones on my street. *Think. Think.* I knew the crosswalk was important. And I hadn't been out on the big main street, where my mommy had pointed out the crosswalk.

I started to walk again. Faster and faster. I had to find the big main street and the crosswalk. There, up ahead, I could see where two streets crossed with each other. *That must be it!* I started to run. I slowed down as I got closer to the next street and stopped when I reached it. I looked up it and then down it. *This isn't it, is it? No, there are just more and more houses.* I started to panic. I needed to get home. I could feel the lump swelling up in my throat. *Wait.* I could see another street about halfway up. *That must be it. I'm sure that's it!*

I ran as fast as I could, up the street to where I was sure I was going to find the big main street with the crosswalk. When I reached it, I looked back and forth, up and down. They all looked the same! Houses, houses and more houses. I looked behind me, in the direction I had just come from. It was all the same. I didn't know what to do. I was lost!

I stood there for a moment as panic took over. Tears welled up in my eyes, the fear gripping me. I was frozen to my spot with this overwhelming urge to run. Anywhere. To just run and run. *But wait. Think. I can do this. I can find my way. I just have to think. Take a deep breath. Think.*

I looked back around. I looked up, down, right and left. *Which way do I go?* I picked a direction that I thought I hadn't tried yet and started to walk. As I walked, I could see another crossroad in the distance. *That's it! It must be. The main street wasn't very far from the school, so it must be somewhere close by,* I reasoned. As my confidence increased, I started to run again. The main street grew closer and closer and I started to run faster and faster. I was almost there. My legs were growing weary and I just wanted to sit right down on the sidewalk, but relief and excitement spurred me on. I started to slow down as I reached the street. And then I stopped and looked up and down, expecting to see the crosswalk.

Nothing. Nothing but houses, houses and more houses. The panic was instant. I had never felt such fear in all my life! *What do I do? Do I try to go back in the direction I started? Do I try to find the school again? So much time has passed. I'm going to be late. My mommy's going to wonder where I am. I'm so scared.* I could feel the tears coming again and the lump swell up in my throat.

Just as I was about to give in to the panic and start to cry, I thought, *no! I will not cry. I am not a baby. I will not cry. What if someone sees me? What if they catch me crying? They'll think I'm a baby for sure. I will not cry. I will not cry. I will not cry.* At that point, I was walking aimlessly, trying to stop myself from crying—trying to control the fear, the panic, the hopelessness of the situation.

As I reached another intersection, I was about to turn right, when for some reason, I turned left instead. I continued to walk along, in kind of a daze.

And then. There it was. The school. *I'm back at the school?* I stood there staring at it for a moment. At first, I was relieved to find something familiar. But then I realized that I had spent all that time wandering and I was no closer to home. I was in big trouble. *Mommy is going to be so mad,* I thought. And then I saw it. The plaza. *The plaza!* I remembered, now, that Mommy had said there was a plaza where we turned in to the street where the school was. So I ran toward it. And there it was! The big main street. And way up ahead, I could see the crosswalk. *The crosswalk! I found it.*

I felt a surge of energy as I started to run with confidence toward the crosswalk. I ran and ran and ran. I ran faster than I had ever run before. The man at the crosswalk put up his sign and all the cars stopped as I ran across the street. The man was telling me not to run, but I did anyway. I just wanted to get home as fast as I could.

Then I saw the other plaza, with the grocery store in it. I was almost there. I kept running and running. I could hardly catch my breath and I had a pain in my side that was getting stronger and stronger. But I kept running. And there it was. I could see it now. My mommy's car in our driveway! I was almost there. I was almost home.

I ran up the driveway and in the side door, hearing the door slam behind me. As I leapt up the stairs and into the kitchen, I heard my big brother Teddy shouting, "She's home, Ma. Joey's home."

My mommy ran into the kitchen yelling, "Where have you been"?

"I got lost," I cried out, as I began to sob uncontrollably. I was so relieved. I'd been so terrified and now I was finally home, where I was safe again.

And then my mommy started to cry. "What am I going to do? I have to get back to work or I'll lose my job. I can't afford to lose my job. We need this job. You need to get your lunch and I can't take the time to drive you back to school. Oh God, what am I going to do?" she cried.

Oh no, what have I done? I thought as I ran into my mommy's arms. "I'm sorry, Mommy. It's okay. I can walk back to school by myself. I know the way now. Honest, Mommy. I can do it. Please don't cry."

And then Teddy was hugging us, too, saying, "Ma, don't worry. I'll walk Jo back to school. I don't mind. And I'll bring her back home again after school. Everything's okay. I'm the man of the house now and I'll take care of her. You just go back to work now, okay? I promise, Ma. It's okay. I'll make sure she eats her lunch and I'll get her back to school."

"Thank you, Ted. You're a good boy." My mommy had finally stopped crying. "I have to go or I'll be late," she added as she wiped her eyes.

I wanted to shout out and reassure them both that I was okay to go back to school by myself, but something stopped me from saying it out loud. *Maybe it'll be okay to walk with Teddy for just this one day. Besides, I love being with my big brother. He's the best.*

When the school day was over, the bell rang and we all filed out of the school. And, true to his word, there was Teddy, waiting outside for me, just as I knew he would be.

A few of his new friends were with him and he casually said, "Come on, Jo, let's go."

"Coming," I sang out, as I hurried to keep up with them.

Some of his new friends started to tease me as we were heading home.

Suddenly, Teddy blurted out, "Leave her alone! No one picks on my little sister, ya hear?"

"Okay, Ted. Sorry about that," they called out.

I felt so proud. Here was my big brother Teddy standing up for me. I knew I would always feel safe as long as he was with me.

Later that day, in the bathroom, I thought about how much I loved my new teacher. Her name was Miss Sommers and she was the nicest teacher I had ever known. I closed my eyes for a moment, thinking about how lucky I was.

Hello, luv. And how are you today?

William! I'm fine! How are you?

We are just wonderful. We couldn't possibly feel any better, at this moment. And how was your first day at school?

*It was great! I have this new teacher and she's just wonderful and Teddy walked me home from school and he made his friends stop teasing me and—*and then I remembered. *I got lost coming home from school at lunchtime. How come you didn't help me find my way home?*

We were with you the whole time. You did just fine. You found your way, didn't you?

Yes, but I was so scared. Why didn't you show me the way?

But we did, dear child.

You did?

Don't you remember? That last turn you made, before finding the school again? You were going to turn the wrong way.

I remember. That was you? I remember that I was going to go one way and all of a sudden, I decided to go the other way instead.

Yes, dear one—that was us. We helped you to go the correct way.

Thank you, William. But—

But what, dear child?

Why didn't you help me right from the start? Why did you let me get lost in the first place?

You need to have your own experiences, little one. It's how you learn and grow. It's how you decide on what you want.

I already know what I want. I don't want to get lost. That's what I want.

That's what you don't want. It isn't what you do want. So tell us, what is it that you do want?

I want to not get lost.

That's still what you don't want.

I huffed and then I thought about it. *I want to always know my way home.*

You've got it! That's perfect. That's exactly what we wish to teach you!

I was a little confused. They acted like I just said the most amazing thing. I could feel their excitement and it made me feel excited too.

You've learned a great lesson today, dear child. We want you to always remember this. We know you don't fully comprehend it yet, but it will serve you well to think about it. We'll talk about it again another time.

I could feel that familiar warmth of love wash over me. I could feel their joy and excitement through my whole body. *I love you, William. I love you so much.*

Our love for you is greater than you know.

I sat there for a moment longer, revelling in the wonderful way I felt. And finally, I got up, washed my hands and left the bathroom, heading into my room, anticipating the exciting life ahead of me.

Chapter 5

I sat thinking in my room, waiting to be called downstairs for supper. I did a lot of that—I liked to think and daydream, as Mommy called it. I thought about things that had already happened and about how I would have liked them to be different. And I thought about the future. Tomorrow, next week, next month. Right now, I was thinking about things that had happened lately. Mommy said that meant I was thinking about the past. I liked thinking about the past, especially the good stuff. It made me feel happy, thinking about happy things that had already happened. Trouble is, it sometimes reminded me of other things that didn't make me feel so good. William says that when that happens, I should try to think about the happy things again so I start to feel good again.

So there I was, thinking and remembering. I hadn't been six years old for very long, and yet so much had happened. My parents had broken up, we'd spent most of the summer at our neighbour's farm, I'd been to three schools and we'd moved to a new home with just our mommy. But all in all, things were okay. Daddy was away on business a lot of the time, so I didn't really notice his absence. The summer at the farm and cottage was wonderful, and our new home was great. I loved my new school, so I was happy about that. There were loads and loads of kids on our new street. There were five kids in my family. This was a lot in our old neighbourhood, but in our new one, we were pretty average. Some families had only two or three kids, but there was a bunch of families that had six, seven or eight kids!

"Dinner's ready," Mommy called out.

I ran downstairs to the kitchen.

It was a typical dinnertime. Mommy had already fed my baby sister, and the rest of us were sitting at the kitchen table. Mommy was eating at the dining room table by herself because there was only room for the four of us at the kitchen table. We didn't mind, though. In fact, it was better. That way we could trade food with each other. There were very few vegetables that I liked, so usually I could trade my veggies for potatoes or meat. And when no one wanted to trade, there was always my big brother, Teddy. He liked everything! And what an appetite. We called him the human garbage disposal.

I looked down at my plate and wrinkled my nose. *Yuk! Canned peas and carrots.* I hated them both.

"Psst, Teddy?" I whispered. I pointed to my peas and carrots.

Teddy lifted his plate over closer to me, so that I could scrape the vegetables onto his plate.

Phew. Thank goodness he's hungry tonight.

Kevin scraped his peas onto Carol's plate and she gave him her carrots.

With everyone satisfied with their new meals, we ate silently for a short while. As we started to get full, we began to joke and nudge and giggle. Some of the remaining food landed on the table, the floor and our clothes—a typical dinnertime.

Once dinner was over and the mess cleaned up, we all scattered to our rooms or the basement to play. It was already dark out, so we weren't allowed to play outside.

"Kids, come in here. Into the living room. I want to talk to you," my mommy called out.

Oh no. Someone's in trouble. Big trouble!

We were not allowed in the living room, and Mommy would call us all together only when there was something wrong. *What could it be?* A sense of foreboding washed over me as I slowly walked down the stairs to the living room. My brothers were already there and I could tell by the looks on their faces that they were thinking the same as me. We looked at each other with questioning faces, wondering what was up. No one seemed to know.

"Come on, Carol. We're all waiting," my mommy called out, as she sat on the arm of the couch.

I was getting more and more frightened while we waited for Carol. Mommy didn't look mad, so that wasn't it. We weren't in trouble. *So what is it?* It was something big. I could tell. I looked at Mommy's face and I became terrified. She looked sad and afraid.

What's going on? Something's wrong. Really, really, wrong. I could feel my face grow warm, and the hairs on my body made my skin tingle. Whatever it was, I didn't want to know. Everyone was quiet.

Carol sauntered into the room and sat down on the floor in front of my mommy.

"Now, kids, I don't want you to be afraid, but Mommy has to go into the hospital for an operation. I have breast cancer and they're going to have to remove one of my breasts."

I didn't know exactly what that meant, but I knew it was serious. Carol started to cry. I turned partially away so no one could see how hard I was trying to stop from crying. I didn't know what was wrong, but it terrified me.

"Quit crying, Carol. Look, you're upsetting Mom," I heard Teddy scolding.

"But I don't want them to cut Mommy's breast off," she wailed.

"It's okay, Carol. I'll be the same person. They need to remove it," my mommy choked out. I could tell she was trying so hard not to cry, just like me.

"It's okay, Ma. You're going to be fine. We love you. I know you're going to be fine," I heard Teddy reassuring her. But it sounded like he was trying to convince himself as well as Mommy.

Fear gripped me, choking me. I held my breath so I wouldn't cry. I looked over at my mommy. Teddy was hugging her and Carol was wrapped around her legs, sobbing.

"You'll be okay, Ma," Teddy said, his voice breaking. He coughed to hide the fact that he was also trying hard not to cry.

I wanted to run away. I was terrified and I just wanted everything to go back to normal.

"I'm so sorry, kids. I didn't mean for this to happen. You need to be strong. I'll do my best to be strong for you," she said, sobbing.

Please let this stop. Please let my mommy be okay. I was starting to feel dizzy from fighting so hard not to cry.

My mommy explained that she would be in the hospital for two weeks, so our father would be looking after us the first week and her girlfriend would come the second. She had gained control of her voice and as she talked about when she would be going into the hospital, her voice started to fade. I no longer heard what she was saying, but I could tell she was still talking. I noticed her tone of voice change and there was movement. She had stood up. Kevin and

Carol were heading to the basement and Teddy was heading toward the stairs. It was over. The talk was over.

I slowly moved toward the stairs to go up to my room. I felt numb—emotionally drained. I still didn't really understand what was happening, but I knew that my mommy was sick and that it was really serious.

I sat in my room feeling frightened. The door was open and then I heard it. My big brother Teddy was in his room with the door closed. At first I wasn't sure what I was hearing. Then I realized he was crying.

As I sat there listening to my brother sobbing, I became terrified. The fear gripped me. *It has to be really bad for Teddy to cry.* I could feel the hairs on my head tingling. A lump formed in my throat and my eyes filled with tears.

I was in a state of panic. I wanted to run away, but there was nowhere to go. I couldn't get away from the fear. I felt helpless as I started to sob. *I have to get away from this.*

I ran out of my bedroom and into the bathroom. *William!* I cried out in my mind. *William, please come.*

Silence.

William, I pleaded. *I need you, William.* The tears poured down my face as I closed my eyes and called out to my friends. *William, please.*

Still—just silence.

William! I'm begging you, please.

Nothing.

Where are they? William, please come. I need you. My mommy is sick.

Nothing.

William, where are you? William, please! Please don't leave me alone!

I opened my eyes and ran to the toilet. I quickly slammed the lid down and sat. I stared at the tiles on the wall, in a panic. I tried to stare at one tile, just like William had taught me to. But I couldn't concentrate. *Please William! I'm begging you. Please help me.*

Nothing.

William, please. My mommy is sick. Please make her better. William. Can't you hear me? Please, William. I'll do anything you ask. I promise. Please help my mommy!

Still nothing.

Where is William? Why don't they come to me? Why are they leaving me all alone and frightened? How could they do this to me? Please, William. I promise I'll be good. Please don't leave me! I need you. My mommy needs you! Please make my mommy better.

I felt so alone. So terrified. I felt my supper rising up in my throat. I was going to be sick. I got off the toilet, lifted the lid and brought up my supper. I flushed the toilet and sat there on the floor. For a few minutes I felt a little better. And then the fear and panic returned.

William. Why won't you come to me? Please, William. You have to help my mommy. I don't want my mommy to die!

And there it was. That's why I felt so terrified. I sensed that my mommy could die. I didn't know exactly what dying was, but I did know that it meant that she would leave and never come back. I couldn't bear the thought that I would never see my mommy again. I felt so alone. I lay down and put my cheek on the cold floor and dozed off. Suddenly, I jerked awake to knocking on the door, and Mommy calling out.

"Joanne, what are you doing in there? Joanne, open the door."

I felt confused. What was happening?

"Joanne. Do you hear me? I said open this door. What are you doing?"

I could hear the concern in my mommy's voice. I got up and unlocked the door.

"What were you doing in here all this time?"

"I fell asleep."

"Asleep? Why would you fall asleep in the bathroom?"

I could hear the relief and confusion in my mommy's voice. "I don't know." My head felt fuzzy and I still felt tired.

"Go get your pyjamas on and get into bed."

I walked into my room in a daze. I put my pyjamas on and crawled into bed. I don't remember anything else, so I must have fallen asleep right away.

Chapter 6

It was just as Mommy had said. Daddy came to look after us the day she went into the hospital. We hadn't seen him since they'd broken up, so at first he was acting pretty nice. He didn't seem to know what most of the rules were, so we managed to get away with a lot more than usual.

On the third day, when we came home from school, I could tell that he'd been cooking. That was very unusual. My mommy had made a number of dinners and frozen them so that my daddy wouldn't need to cook. She said he didn't know how to cook and that she wanted us to eat properly while she was away. The smell of curry filled the house as I walked through the door. I liked curry. Mommy made it really good with chicken pieces and pineapple chunks over rice. *Mmm.*

But then I noticed that something smelled different about it. I wasn't quite sure what was different, but that was okay. Curry was curry, and I liked curry.

We were all seated at the table for dinner when I discovered the difference in the curry. I took one big mouthful and started to chew. *Ew, yuk.* I spit it out onto the plate. I looked around as my brothers and sister did the same.

"You eat every last bit of it!" my father bellowed at us.

My whole body jerked at the sound.

"I slaved all afternoon over this meal and there's nothing wrong with it. You all love curry and you'll all eat it up. There's nothing else to eat, so get to it." He was really mad.

"But it tastes awful. We don't like it. You didn't make it like Mom does," both my brothers complained.

"Yeah," I chimed in.

"Eat it. There's not a damn thing wrong with it! I don't give a shit how your mother makes it. You'll eat it and you'll do it now," he bellowed, getting madder and madder. He grabbed his own plate and stormed into the dining room to eat. "Fuck. This tastes like shit! God damn it. God, fuckin' damn it," he grumbled, as he stormed back in the kitchen and dumped his dinner in the garbage.

"See, we told you. It's awful. We don't have to eat it, do we? Please," Teddy chimed in.

"Yes, you do have to eat it! Now, get to it. I don't want to hear another word out of you until it's all gone," he shouted.

"But—"

"And that goes for all of you," he warned as he stormed out.

It took us all over an hour to eat as much as we could, gagging with every mouthful. I was so angry. *It isn't fair. He didn't like it either, but he's still making us eat it.* I had forgotten how mean my father could be.

It turned out he'd used grapefruit in the curry instead of pineapple. Yuk! I got up from the table and went upstairs to the bathroom. I sat there, going to the bathroom, with very little on my mind. About the only thing I was feeling was the relief that I had finally finished that horrible supper.

Hello, luv.

It was William! I felt a mixture of excitement, relief, confusion and anger. *William! Where have you been?*

We've been here all along, dear child.

No you weren't. I came looking for you and you wouldn't come to me! I really needed you and you left me alone.

Dear, dear, little one. Don't you know that we would never abandon you?

What does abandon *mean?*

It means that we would never leave you alone. Desert you.

But you did! You did leave me alone.

Dear, dear sweet little child. We have always been here. You just couldn't hear us.

Why not? Why couldn't I hear you? I needed you so badly and you weren't here!

But we were, precious one. We were calling to you but you just couldn't hear. You see, you were feeling so bad—so desperate— that you didn't have access to us.

I don't understand.

You needed to quiet your mind, as we've taught you to do. Then you would have heard us.

But I tried and it didn't work. I was too frightened to concentrate. But I tried really, really hard!

We know, precious one. That was the problem. You were trying and trying and trying. You mustn't try so hard. If you just relax, still your mind and have faith that we will be here, then we will be.

William had explained to me many times before that I should take deep breaths and quiet my mind. If I was able to quiet my mind then they would be able to talk to me.

My thoughts jumped ahead. *Do you know that my mommy is sick? She's in the hospital having an operation.*

We know, little one.

Is she going to be okay? Can you help her get better?

Of course we can help her.

I started to feel excited. A huge sense of relief came over me. *Oh, thank you, William! I knew you could. I just knew it!*

Now, just so we're clear, your mother has to do her part.

I don't understand. What do you mean? I thought you could just use your magic to make her better.

We can. As long as your mother has faith that she will get better.

I'll tell her about you. I'll explain to her that she has to believe and she will get better. Once she knows, she will believe.

Good girl. You know, it is also important that you believe. You must have faith that everything will work out exactly as it should.

Oh, I do! I do!

We know you do. You must always remember, no matter what. Even if it sometimes doesn't seem as though it is true. Do you understand?

I think so.

Even when things appear to be going wrong, you must always have faith that everything will work out perfectly.

I will, I promise.

I felt that familiar warmth washing over me. Filling me up with their love. I felt so strong. So sure. I knew that my mommy was going to be okay. *I love you so much, William. Thank you. I'm so glad you're here.*

Our love for you is greater than you know.

And with that, I got up and left the bathroom, feeling better than I had ever felt before.

Chapter 7

I woke to the warmth of the sun beaming down on me through the bedroom window. I felt really good that morning. Lately, I was waking up with a sense of panic or doom, ever since Mommy had told us she was sick. But not that morning. As I got out of my bed, I suddenly had an idea. I felt excited with the anticipation. Today was going to be a wonderful day. I ran over to my closet and opened the door. The excitement was building. *Where is it?* I searched through the clothes in my closet. *There it is!* I grabbed the hanger and pulled it out of the closet. It was wrapped in a special plastic bag to keep it clean and safe. I laid it on my bed and started to unzip the bag. Again, I felt my excitement building.

"Joanne. Carol. Breakfast is ready. Hurry up and get down here," my daddy called from the kitchen.

I froze. *Oh no, what should I do?* I stared down at the bag. *I don't want Carol to see it. What if she comes back into our room?*

Then I heard the bathroom door open and I could hear Carol running down the stairs.

"Joanne. I said get down here!" my father shouted again.

"Coming," I called. I needed time to think. I grabbed the blanket from my bed and pulled it down to cover the bag. I stood back to see if it was totally hidden. It was.

"Joanne!"

"Coming," I shouted as I opened the bedroom door and ran down the stairs, two at a time. *Whoa!* I started to slip. I reached out and grabbed the handrail. Without missing a beat, I used the rail to push me off the stairs and down the final three steps.

I sat down at the table and started to eat the porridge he had set out for me. *Yuk!* It was thick, pasty and lumpy. But I didn't care. I just wanted to eat it as quickly as I could and get back upstairs before Carol finished hers.

I managed to empty the bowl and the glass of orange juice in record time. I even finished before my brothers were done. And they'd started before me! I grabbed the bowl and glass and ran to the sink. I filled the bowl with cold water, just like I had done most mornings, and ran out of the kitchen and up the stairs.

"Don't forget to brush your teeth and wash your face," my father called out to me.

"Okay, I will," I called out as I ran into the bedroom and closed the door.

For once, I was glad that Carol was such a slow, picky eater. *If I hurry, I should be done before she comes back up.*

I uncovered the bag, finished unzipping it and stood back to admire it. I could feel my excitement build as I stared down at it. I quickly stripped out of my pyjamas and threw them on the bed. I put on my undies and tights, trying to be as quiet as I could. I needed to keep an ear to the stairs, so that I would have some warning if Carol came up. I carefully slipped it on and ran out of the room and into my mommy's room. My mommy has a full length mirror on the back of her door and I wanted to get a full view of myself. I stood back to see the full effect. I was so pleased. Again, I felt the excitement well up in me. I looked wonderful. I could feel the pride swelling up in me as I stared at myself in the mirror. And there, staring back at me was the fanciest party dress I had ever owned!

A friend of my mommy's had given Carol and me the most beautiful party dresses. So far, I had not had a chance to wear mine. It was pale yellow, which Mommy said looked really good with my bright red hair. I never understood why people always said my hair was red—it wasn't. It was bright orange! Like a carrot. *Why didn't they say it was orange?*

The dress had an outer layer of sheer material and an underneath layer of shiny satin material. Then, best of all, it also had another underneath layer that was separate. *What did Mommy say it was called? Oh yeah. It's a crinoline.* It's like a slip, only it has a hoop in the hem of it that makes the dress flare out all around. I looked like a fairy princess.

Then suddenly I remembered—I had almost forgotten the best part! I ran back into my room and into the closet. I pulled the box out from the floor of the closet and opened it.

And there they were! A beautiful pair of shiny, black, patent leather shoes. I slipped them on and noticed that they had become a little tight on me.

That's okay. They're not too bad.

"Come on, Joanne. It's time to go," my father shouted from downstairs.

Where is Carol? I didn't see or hear her come up to get dressed. Maybe she came up when I was in Mommy's room. That must be it.

"Get a move on. We're going to be late."

"Coming," I shouted, as I carefully and slowly made my way down the stairs.

"What the hell is that?" my daddy bellowed as I walked into the kitchen.

"It's my party dress," I said, glowing with pride.

"I can see that. What the hell are you doing with it on? Jesus Christ, I don't have time for this shit!"

"I'm allowed to wear it. We're having a party at school today," I lied.

"How come I never heard about a party?" Carol jumped in.

"It's only in my class," I answered, glaring at Carol.

Why can't Carol mind her own business? She's always poking her nose into everyone else's business. I was angry at Carol, but I was more nervous about my father finding out that I had lied to him.

"All right, let's go. You're going to be late if we don't get a move on."

Phew! What a relief. That went better than I thought it would.

I ran outside to the car to avoid any further discussion about my dress. I opened the back door and tried to jump in the car. *Shoot.* The hoop was catching on the opening. I didn't want to bend the hoop, so I had to figure out how to get in the car without damaging it. Both my brothers snickered at me.

"Shut up," I huffed, as I tried different angles to get in. I needed to get in the car before my daddy came out or he might make me change out of my dress.

I finally managed to squeeze the hoop just enough to get it in the door without doing any damage to it. I sat down on the back seat and the dress flew up and covered my face. My brothers were laughing out loud now. And I was getting angry. I pushed the hoop forward and held it there, as Carol and my daddy came out to the car.

So I just held it there like that, for the whole ride to school. I was very careful to get out of the car with as little fussing as I could. I didn't want my daddy to see me having any difficulty.

Once I got out of the car and headed to the schoolyard toward my friends, I started to get excited again. I couldn't wait to show them my beautiful dress and shoes. Some of the boys giggled and laughed, but I didn't care. The girls all admired my outfit and commented on how wonderful I looked. And I felt wonderful! It was even better than I had imagined it would be. I felt so special. So pretty. I liked having all that attention.

The bell rang, so we all moved over and lined up outside the school doors. I had to be especially careful in the lineup as I didn't want anyone crushing my hoop. When I arrived at the door to my classroom, I made sure I was positioned in the centre of the entrance so I wouldn't brush against the sides and get my dress dirty. The hoop barely fit through the doorway, but I managed to get through it without touching the sides.

As I entered the class, I caught my teacher's eye. She had a surprised look on her face.

"Good morning, Miss Sommers," I sang, as I broke out into a huge smile.

"My, my, Joanne. That is a lovely dress!"

"Thank you, Miss Sommers." I beamed. I felt so pleased that she liked my dress.

"May I ask what the special occasion is?"

"I didn't have anything else to wear. All the rest of my clothes are in the laundry," I fibbed. *It's just a little fib. I'm not hurting anyone.*

"Well, I'm not sure it's the most practical outfit for school, but go ahead and get seated," she said sweetly.

When I arrived at my desk, I realized I was facing another challenge. I stared at the chair attached to my desk and tried to figure out how I was going to sit down without damaging my dress. I turned sideways and eased my way into and down onto my chair. The hoop went flying up in the air, covering my face. I heard the class laughing. I was so embarrassed. I quickly stood up and tried to figure out another way to do this. I studied the desk and chair. *How can I make this work? There has to be a way.* And then I had an idea.

I bent my knees so that the hoop was lying underneath the desk and then I slowly eased my way back over to the chair and sat down. This time the hoop came flying up behind me! The whole class started to laugh. I looked up at my teacher and caught her trying to hide her laughter.

I felt my face burning with embarrassment. Tears welled up in my eyes. I heard my classmates laugh and, before I realized what was happening, I burst out laughing myself. I finally realized that maybe it hadn't been such a good idea to wear my party dress to school after all. *But I'm here now. What am I supposed to do for the rest of the day?* "Perhaps it might be better if you went home and changed?" my teacher suggested, as if reading my mind.

"Yes, Miss Sommers," I replied as I got up from my desk and slowly shuffled to the classroom door, my shoulders slumped, head bent.

As I left the classroom, I was already planning the story I would tell my father when I got home. He would be furious if he knew I had lied to him. I had to come up with something he would believe.

I started to run out of the schoolyard but the hoop made my dress bounce up and down with each step I took, so I held the dress and walked as quickly as possible all the way home.

As I opened the side door and slowly entered the house, I saw my father standing there.

"I knew you were lying! You told me there was a party today. Your teacher called me and told me there was no party! How dare you embarrass me like that," he hollered.

"I didn't lie. I made a mistake," I cried out, trying to lessen his anger. "I thought we were having a party today. I made a mistake. Honest. I thought today was a party day."

"Get upstairs and get that damn thing off and get dressed for school," he yelled, as he raised his hand to hit me.

I ducked and ran past him. As I carefully shuffled up the stairs, I thought, *Phew, that wasn't so bad.* I ran into my mommy's room and took one last look at myself in the mirror.

I gazed at my beautiful dress. *It was worth it. I got to wear this magical dress, and who cares that I couldn't wear it all day. I still got to wear it for part of the day. I got to be a fairy princess and it made me feel so wonderful. It was definitely worth it.* I smiled as I walked back into my bedroom to change.

After I changed into my regular school clothes, I thought I'd better try to go to the bathroom before heading back to school. As I sat there remembering how beautiful I looked in my party dress, I glowed with satisfaction.

Top of the morning to you, dear child. And how are you on this fine day?

I beamed. *William. It's so good to hear from you! I feel great! I got to wear my party dress to school today. And all my girlfriends loved it.*

We know, little one. We are very pleased that you are so happy.

Oh, I am. I am. I just love my party dress. It's the best thing I own. I wanted so much to wear it, but I haven't had a party to go to ever since I got it. I looked so beautiful in it. You should have seen me!

We can feel your joy. And your joy is our joy. We are truly pleased.

I felt like I would explode with the joy and pride I felt. I could not stop smiling. I could feel William's joy for me as well. I felt their love and joy for me. And it made me feel even better than I ever thought was possible.

I love you so much, William!

Our love for you is greater than you know.

It was the first time ever that I felt like I truly understood what they meant by that.

And my love for you is greater than you know.

The glow of love and joy stayed with me as I left the bathroom and went downstairs to go back to school.

Chapter 8

The second week started out great. My mommy's girlfriend Norma was really nice. And funny, too! She was always cracking jokes and laughing. And she loved to sing. Funny songs.

She told us that Mommy was doing well and that we would be seeing her soon. She did warn us, though, that Mommy would still feel sick for a while after she got home, so we would have to be quiet and good for her.

I can do that. I was really looking forward to seeing my mommy. They wouldn't let us visit her in the hospital and I really missed her.

It was Saturday, and Mommy was coming home on Tuesday. We were all getting excited to see her. The past two weeks had felt like an eternity. I was eating a sandwich at the kitchen table when Teddy came home. Norma had sent him to the store for milk, bread and cigarettes.

"The man at the store wouldn't give me the cigarettes. He said I need a note from you to buy them," Teddy told Norma as he put the bread and milk away.

"Okay, grab me a piece of paper and I'll write one for you," she replied.

Teddy got her a piece of paper and pen. She wrote the note and handed it to him.

"You can spend ten cents on yourself, seeing as how you have to make a second trip. Now hurry up. I'm dying for a smoke," she said as she started to pace the floor.

"But I need more money," Teddy piped up.

"What do you mean, you need more money? I gave you four dollars already! Where's my change from the milk and bread?"

"This is all I have," Teddy answered, holding out his hand with some coins in it.

"Where's the other dollar? There should be another dollar! What did you do with it?" she demanded.

"This is all they gave me back," Teddy said, still holding out his hand.

Norma grabbed the coins and counted them.

"That's impossible. There should be another dollar. You spent it, didn't you?" she accused.

"No, I didn't. This is all they gave me," Teddy urged, his voice cracking.

"You little liar! You're a thief! That was all the money I had. What am I going to do now? You give me my money, right now," she demanded.

"I don't have it," Teddy cried.

I couldn't believe what I was seeing and hearing. *How can Norma say that Teddy stole her money? Teddy would never steal anything. And he would never lie about it either!*

When I saw my big brother crying and pleading with her to believe him, I could feel a lump forming in my throat.

"You little liar. How could you steal from me and then lie about it? You selfish little bastard! How dare you. Your mother's in the hospital dying and I'm looking after you out of the goodness of my heart. And you have the gall to steal my last dollar? How could you?" she screamed, getting louder and louder.

"I didn't steal anything," he sobbed as he turned and ran down the stairs.

"My brother doesn't steal. And he doesn't lie! I don't like you anymore. You're mean and you're a liar. Teddy didn't steal your stupid money," I shouted as the anger swelled up in me.

I turned and ran down the stairs to the basement to find my brother. "Teddy, I believe you. I know you didn't steal her money," I assured him. "She's a mean old witch. And she's the liar," I continued.

And then it struck me. *What did she mean when she said that Mommy was dying?* Terror gripped me instantly. *No, it's not true! It isn't true. It can't be true.* I couldn't bear to even think about it, so I focused on the lost money.

"Want me to go back to the store and look for it? I'll find it," I continued, trying to make Teddy feel better. He had stopped crying and had become really quiet. *Had he remembered the same thing I had? Was he thinking about Mommy?*

"No, I'll go," he blurted out. I could hear the panic in his voice.

Yes, he remembered.

He got up and ran up the stairs and out the door and I ran after him.

I didn't want to think. I just wanted to be with my brother. Help him. I wanted to find the money and make him feel better. And I didn't want to think. I couldn't think about it. About Mommy.

We ran all the way back to the store. I was looking down at the ground as we ran, hoping to see the dollar. When we arrived at the store, I stayed outside, looking all around, still convinced that I would spot the money on the ground and save the day!

Suddenly, Teddy came running out of the store, waving two packages of cigarettes in his hands.

"I got the cigarettes," he announced excitedly.

"The man in the store had kept the money for the cigarettes, expecting me to come right back with the note," he explained.

He sounded relieved. I was so happy for my brother. We ran even faster, all the way home. I knew he couldn't wait to get home and tell Norma what had really happened. We both knew that Norma would be pleased. *Everything is working out okay after all*. We ran and ran.

And we were right. Norma was thrilled! She kept saying how sorry she was for accusing Teddy of stealing. She hugged him and told him she didn't mean all the things she had said.

And then I remembered again.

And so did Teddy. He suddenly grew stiff and quiet. He pulled away from Norma's arms.

Panic gripped me instantly. *No, it's not true!* I demanded silently. I felt the hairs on my body stand out as I silently pleaded.

Norma must have noticed the change in us. "Hey, you guys, what's up?" she asked, with a confused look on her face.

"What you said about Mom. Did you mean it?" Teddy asked, his voice cracking, pleading.

Norma's face turned red. She looked shocked and guilty as she reassured us.

"I shouldn't have said that. Your mom is going to be okay. I was just so mad. I didn't mean it. Honest. She's going to be fine. You'll see. She'll be fine," she kept saying.

I wanted so much to believe her, but I just couldn't be sure. She had a strange look on her face and she didn't really sound like she was telling the truth. She was just trying to make us feel better.

I could tell that Teddy wasn't convinced either. He slowly moved toward the stairs and I followed him.

I knew that Teddy was feeling just as terrified as I was. *My mommy has to be okay. She's all we have. We love her. We need her. She has to be okay!*

I followed Teddy up the stairs.

"Mommy's going to be okay, Teddy. I just know it. Don't listen to her. She doesn't know what she's talking about. Mommy's going to be fine."

"I don't want to talk about it. Just leave me alone!" He ran into his room and slammed the door.

I went into my room and threw myself on the bed. I curled up in a ball and started to cry. As I lay there crying, I thought I heard William calling to me, reminding me of a conversation we had not that long ago. *William! Yes, of course. I need to talk to William. They will make me feel better.* I was sure of it!

I got up and ran into the bathroom. I closed and locked the door.

Just take it easy. Relax. You need to quiet your mind, like William explained.

And just like I had done so many times before, I sat down on the toilet lid and looked at the tiles on the wall. I stared at one of them and started to breathe deeply. Slow, deep breaths. And I stared and stared.

At first it wasn't working, but I kept breathing deeply and staring.

Good afternoon, luv. What a glorious day it is. Don't you agree?

I'm afraid, William.

And why are you afraid, dear child?

'Cause Norma says my mommy is dying.

And what do you believe?

My brother is afraid that she's dying too.
And what do you believe?
I don't know what to believe.
You need to think about it. How do you feel? Do you believe that your mother is dying?
You told me that everything was going to be okay. You said that you would help my mommy!
And what else did we tell you?
Umm. I'm not sure. I don't remember.
You remember. Think. What else did we say?
You said that Mommy had to believe that she would get better. Yes and what else?
And then I remembered. *You said that I had to believe.*
That's right. And what else?
My mind was struggling to remember. *What else did they say? I remember! You said that no matter what happens, I had to continue to have faith that my mommy would get better!*
And do you have faith? Do you believe that your mother will get better? Do you believe that everything will happen just as it should?
I want to.
Well that's a start. But do you believe? Do you trust that everything will work out perfectly?
I think I do. Yes, I do. I trust you. You said it will be okay, so I believe it will be okay!
There you go. That's it, dear child. You've got it! We are very pleased that you have remembered.
I started to feel better. After all, I really did trust William. *They would never lie to me. They said that everything would be okay, so it will be. I just know it!*
It felt like a big smile had wrapped itself around me and inside me. I could feel that wonderful, familiar feeling of love, filling me with a knowing. Sureness. Happiness. Joy!
I felt so grateful that William had come into my life. *I'm so lucky.*
Thank you for reminding me. I love you, William.
Our love for you is greater than you know.

As I walked out of the bathroom, I thought about telling Teddy about William. I thought about telling him that everything was going to work out perfectly. Just like William said. But something stopped me. I wasn't quite sure, but I thought it might be William. For some reason, I sensed that they didn't want me to tell Teddy about them. Not just now, anyway. This wasn't the right time. So I didn't. That was okay, though. *Everything's going to be just great. I just know it!*

I ran downstairs and shouted, "I'm going out to play!" as I rushed out the door.

It was finally Tuesday morning and I had woken up earlier than usual. I was excited. Mommy was coming home from the hospital today! We all wanted to stay home from school so we could be here when she first got home, but we weren't allowed to. Norma said that Mommy would feel tired and weak when she first got home and that she would need her rest. I couldn't wait for the day to be over, so that I could see my mommy. I missed her so much. I hoped we were going to do interesting things at school today, so that the time would go by faster.

I got up and dressed and went downstairs for breakfast. Norma was just putting the oatmeal out in the bowls.

"I'll do that," I offered, and I grabbed one of the bowls of oatmeal and took it to the table.

Then I came back for another.

"Well, thank you, Joanne. That's very good of you to help."

"You're welcome," I sang out, and I took another bowl to the table.

I put the last bowl down in my spot and sat down to eat.

"Breakfast is ready," Norma called out to everyone.

This would normally be the time that I would come running down to eat, still in my pyjamas. But not today!

I gobbled up my breakfast and gulped down my orange juice. I was almost finished when Kevin and Carol came down to the kitchen in their pyjamas. Teddy arrived a few seconds later, already dressed. And I knew why. He was just as anxious to see Mommy as I was. Kevin and Carol were excited, too; they were just slower to get up and dressed.

As soon as I was finished, I jumped up from the table, put my bowl in the sink and filled it with cold water. Just like Mommy had taught me to—the cold water made it easier to clean the bowl. Usually, we had to use hot water to soak our dirty dishes. But not with oatmeal. It was different.

I ran upstairs and into the bathroom to wash my face and brush my teeth. Once I finished in the bathroom, I went into my room and made my bed.

I don't normally make my bed on a school day, but today I wanted Mommy to be happy when she got home. *I know she will be happy to see that I made my bed.* Besides, it was too early to leave for school, and I needed to keep busy so the time would go by fast.

I still left for school earlier than usual. Teddy had left before me. Kevin and Carol were still getting ready. I started to run and then I thought, *Slow down. It's still early. Just take your time.* I was hoping some of my classmates would already be there, but I didn't want to get there too early.

When I rounded the last corner and headed into the schoolyard, I could see that some of my friends were already there after all. What a relief!

Some of the day went more slowly than I had hoped, but fortunately, some of it also went by faster. Finally, it was over. The bell rang and I couldn't get out of there fast enough.

"Hey, Joanne. Want to walk home with us?" some of my friends called out.

"I can't. I'm in a hurry. I have to get home. My mommy got home from the hospital today," I called back to them.

I ran most of the way home. I flew in the door and called out to my mommy.

"I'm home. Where are you, Mommy?"

"I'm up here. In my room."

She sounded strange. It was her voice but she sounded different. I started to feel a little nervous as I slowed down going up the stairs.

When I got to the top of the stairs, I saw that Teddy was already there. He was standing at the door to Mommy's room. He turned to look at me and I stopped dead in my tracks. He looked scared. And I could tell that he'd been crying.

What's going on? What's wrong? I walked over to the bedroom door and then I saw. Mommy looked awful. Really, really sick. I had never seen her look so bad. My mommy is really pretty and she always looks so good. But standing there, looking at her lying in bed, I saw that she looked bad. My heart sank. I felt frightened.

And then I remembered what William had said. They said that I had to believe, no matter what. I had to have faith that everything was going to work out perfectly.

I took a deep breath and walked slowly over to the bed. I wanted to throw myself in her arms, but I was afraid it might hurt her. So I just stood at the side of the bed and touched her bare arm gently.

"I missed you, Mommy. Are you alright?" I asked quietly.

"I'm just a little tired right now. But I'll be alright soon."

But her voice didn't sound convincing. She didn't really believe that she was going to be okay.

"I know you will, Mommy. Everything's going to be just fine. You're going to get all better. But you have to believe it, too. You have to have faith that you will get better and then you will."

She suddenly had a shocked look on her face. Then her face changed to confusion and amazement. "That's exactly what your Grampa says."

I was pleased.

"Where did you hear that from?"

"My secret friends told me."

"What do you mean, secret friends?"

"They're kinda . . . invisible. I can only see them when I close my eyes. And I don't hear them with my ears. I hear them with my mind."

She started to look disappointed, so I continued trying to convince her. "They said you have to think you're going to get better. You have to really believe it. And if you really believe it, then you will get better. Please, Mommy, you have to believe!"

She looked confused and surprised again. "Your Grampa calls it 'mind over matter.' He's been telling me the same thing. You know how smart your Grampa is. So I've been trying to believe. But how could you know such grown-up things?"

I could tell she wasn't really asking me. It was more like she was talking to herself. I was pleased that Grampa had told her the same thing. I sensed that she would find it easier to trust Grampa rather than William. After all, she didn't know William. And I knew that she really looked up to Grampa. She always talked about how much she admired him. That meant she thought he was smart and he knew a lot and she trusted him to tell her what was right.

"Do you believe you are going to get better, Mommy?" I took a deep breath. I was afraid of what her answer might be.

"Of course I do, honey. Grampa says I will and your friends say I will, so I will."

"I know you will get better. I just know it! But you have to really, really, really believe, Mommy. Please, Mommy, believe. Believe with all your heart! I love you, Mommy, and I want you to get better, okay?"

"I will, honey."

"Promise?"

"I promise. Now can you go and play for now? Mommy's feeling tired and I need to rest, if I'm going to get better."

"Okay, Mommy." I walked over to the door where Teddy was still standing. He looked relieved.

"Can you close the door and keep the noise down while I'm resting?"

"Okay, Mommy, I will." I closed the door as I left the room.

"That was a nice thing you told Mom. I think it made her feel better. She looks a little better now, don't you think?" Teddy said.

I could tell he really wanted to believe, too.

"She's just tired right now. She'll feel better after a nap," I reassured him, trying to convince myself as much as Teddy.

We walked quietly downstairs to make sure that Kevin and Carol didn't make any noise when they came in from school.

Chapter 9

As the days turned into weeks and the weeks turned into months, Mommy seemed to be taking forever to get better. She was still tired and weak a lot of the time, and I could hear her crying in bed at night. I felt frightened when I heard her cry. I knew it meant she didn't really believe. That she was afraid. And that made me afraid. I reminded her several times about believing. And each time I did, she seemed to be a little better for a while.

It was Saturday morning and I had just put my sweater on to go out and play.

"I don't want you going out to play yet," Mommy called from the dining room. Her voice sounded better than I had heard it in a long time.

"How come?"

"Uncle Johnny's coming to visit!"

"He is? Oh, goodie! When is he coming?"

"He should be here within the hour, and I don't want you getting dirty before he gets here."

Uncle Johnny wasn't our real uncle. Mommy said that when you have a really close friend of the family, it is a sign of respect to call the person aunt or uncle. It lets people know how much they mean to you and that you consider them a part of the family.

Uncle Johnny is wonderful. We don't see him very often because he is in the navy. He goes away a lot on ships. He travels all over the world. But whenever he comes to visit, we always have such a good time. He is the biggest man I know. He actually has to duck when he goes through a doorway. Honest! And he has the jolliest laugh I have ever heard. He is always so kind to us, and you can tell that he's always so happy to see us. We all love Uncle Johnny.

I was so excited that he was coming. I didn't even mind that I couldn't go out to play. Seeing Uncle Johnny was so much better than going out to play. *But a whole hour? What am I going to do for a whole hour?* Then I had a thought.

"Can we play dress-up with Shirley?"

"Yeah, can we, Mom?" Carol joined in.

"Only if she wants to. And you have to be careful. I don't want you hurting your little sister. She's just a baby."

"We won't, Mommy. We'll be careful. She'll like it," I reassured her as I went running upstairs to get Shirley and some of her clothes.

I ran into my room to look for Shirley. The three of us girls shared a room together. She was sitting up on her bed, playing with a doll.

"Do you want to play dress-up, Shirley?"

"Yeah!" she squealed.

"Okay, let me find some clothes and we'll play down in the basement."

I looked through the closet and started picking out the nicest clothes she had. Shirley was almost three and she was the most beautiful little girl I had ever seen. She had light blond, wavy hair and the most angelic face. People were always giving Mommy beautiful dresses for Shirley, so she had a lot to choose from. Once I'd filled my arms with as many clothes as I could carry, I called out to Shirley to follow me.

When we got to the basement, I put the clothes on the couch and picked out the prettiest dress to put on her. Once she was dressed, I stood back to admire her.

"You look beautiful, Shirley! Come look in the mirror."

I stood behind her and guided her over to the mirror. *She really is beautiful.* "Look at you! You look like a princess. And what a beautiful dress that is. Don't you just love it?"

She looked so pleased with herself. And I felt so pleased with myself. I had picked the perfect dress!

As we stood there admiring the dress and how beautiful Shirley looked in it, I heard a knock at the door.

"It's Uncle Johnny!" I shouted as I bolted up the stairs. "Uncle Johnny's here!" I shouted, reaching the door first.

I yanked the door open and there he was, standing there with a big smile on his face. I moved away from the entrance so he could come in.

"Look how big you've grown! So, do you have a big hug for me?"

He held out his arms and I jumped into them.

"Uncle Johnny, you're here! We were waiting for you."

"Give him a chance to get in the door," I heard my mommy say from the kitchen. But I noticed she had a pleasant tone in her voice. I looked up at her and she was smiling. It had been such a long time since I had seen her smile. Just seeing that smile on her face made her look so much better. *She's getting better. She's going to get completely better, I just know it!*

Uncle Johnny gave Mommy a gentle hug, held her out from him as he studied her face and said, "How are you feeling?"

"It's so good to see you," she said, sighing, and she sank into his arms.

"Why don't I give the kids their gifts and then we'll have a nice talk? What do ya say?"

"That sounds good. I'm so glad you're here!"

"Come on, kids. I have something for each of you," he called out as he headed down the stairs to the basement. Uncle Johnny had brought each of us a real sailor hat. They were amazing! I loved mine and I could tell that everyone else loved theirs, too.

"Now why don't you go out and show your friends your new hats, while I go and visit with your mom for a while. We can spend time together a little later. How does that sound?"

"That sounds good, Uncle Johnny. Thank you for the hats, Uncle Johnny." We were all talking over each other.

I wanted to stay home and spend time with him, but I also knew that Mommy wanted some grown-up time alone with him. She hadn't seen him since before she got sick, and I knew they wanted to talk about it. So we all went out to play.

When we came back in for lunch, we all decided to stay home and visit with Uncle Johnny. It was a wonderful afternoon, talking, joking, playing, wrestling and having so much fun.

We all got to eat supper at the dining room table that night. Normally, we ate in the dining room only at Easter, Thanksgiving and Christmas—when we had turkey. We didn't have turkey, but it still felt like one of those special occasions.

While we were eating, Mommy and Uncle Johnny told us they were going to go on a trip to Virginia Beach in a couple of weeks.

"What's Virginia Beach?" I asked.

"Virginia Beach is this lovely vacation spot. It's right on the Atlantic Ocean and I want to take your mom there so she can get better faster," Uncle Johnny explained.

"Why will Mommy get better faster there?" Teddy asked the question I was thinking.

"Because it is a special place. It's a place that a lot of sick people go to get well," he answered. "It's kind of magic."

"What do you mean, magic?" Teddy asked.

"It has this special energy and it's supposed to heal people," Mommy chimed in.

I looked around the table at my brothers and sister. They all looked confused, just like me.

"You want me to be healed, don't you?"

"Of course we do," we all reassured her.

"But who will look after us when you're away?" Carol asked.

"Grandma is going to come and stay with you. We'll only be gone a week, so you'll barely notice that I'm not here."

"Grandma is coming to stay here?" I asked in surprise.

Grandma and Grampa never came to visit us here. We always went to visit them at the store. They owned a small grocery store attached to their house, and they usually couldn't get away to come and visit.

"Yes, she is. Grampa says it's very important that I go and visit this special place, so Grandma has agreed to come and look after you kids here. It's important that you go to school while I'm away, so it's easier if Grandma comes here."

"This is really important for your mom, kids. I know how much you love her and how much you want her to get well. This is really going to help her get better, and I know you're going to help your grandma look after your baby sister and take care of the house. Right, kids?" Johnny asked.

"I'll do it, Uncle Johnny," Teddy jumped in. "I'll help Grandma look after things. I'll make sure they all go to school and behave themselves. I can even stay home and help Grandma with the housework."

"That would be great if you helped your grandma, Teddy. But you still need to go to school. Your mom will feel so much better if she knows you're going to school. And I know she'll feel good if she knows you're helping your grandma with everything."

Teddy sat up straighter at the table and beamed.

After supper was finished, we all helped clear the table and do the dishes. Then we spent the rest of the evening playing games at the dining room table, just like we always did at Christmas.

That night, I fell asleep to the sounds of Mommy and Uncle Johnny talking quietly downstairs. I couldn't hear what they were saying, but every once in a while, I heard them laughing. It felt so good to hear my mommy laugh again.

When I woke the next morning, I knew that Uncle Johnny had gone. I lay there in bed, thinking about the day before, a smile on my face. I got up and went into the bathroom.

As I sat there feeling happy and content, I stared over at the wall in front of me.

Well, good morning to you, luv. And how are you feeling on this glorious day?

William! It's you! I wasn't even trying to talk to you.

Yes, we know. That makes it so much easier for us to connect with you.

What do you mean?

You remember that we explained that, when you are desperate to speak to us, you have to relax, breathe and quiet your mind to hear us clearly?

Yes, I remember.

Well, you were already in that calm, relaxed state, so it was easy for us to come through.

I was enjoying thinking about what a good time I had yesterday.

Yes, we know. And we are so pleased.

I was wondering, though. I paused.

Yes, go on.

My mommy's going to Virginia Beach to get better. Her and Uncle Johnny say that it's magic there. Is it really magic there?

There is magic everywhere, dear child.

Yes, but they said that this is a special place that will heal my mommy.

And it will.

It will? Oh, that makes me so happy to hear!

You should not have had any doubt. We have talked about this before.

Yes, but you said that Mommy would get better as long as she believed she would get better.

And that is the truth.

But then, which is it? Will my mommy get better if she believes or will she get better if she goes to Virginia Beach?

Yes.

Yes, what?

They are the same thing.

I don't understand.

Do you think that your mother believes that she will be healed by going to this place?

Yes. She sounded really happy when she talked about going.

It does not matter why she believes. It only matters that she believes.

So does that mean it isn't really a magic place?

Of course it is magic. Is it not magical that your mother has finally come to truly believe in her wellness?

Yes, I suppose so. I'm just a little confused still.

Belief in your well-being is very magical, indeed.

So should I tell my mommy that the real magic is in her belief?

Do you think she might doubt her belief, if you tell her that?

She might. I don't want that to happen!

Then it is better if she continues to believe, don't you think?

Oh yes! Then I had a thought. *She will get better, won't she?*

As we have already told you, everything is going to work out perfectly. Do you believe that?

Yes, I do. Well, most of the time.

Whenever you have any doubts, just think about what we said. Remind yourself that everything is going to be just perfect. Do you think you can do that?

Yes, I can do that. I sometimes do that already.

We know you do. You are doing very well and we are extremely pleased.

And there it was! That wonderful, familiar warmth washing over me, filling me up with their love. Making me feel so special, so cherished, so loved. I felt such joy and love for my treasured friends. *Thank you, William. I love you so much!*

Our love for you is greater than you know.

I left the bathroom feeling like I was walking on a cloud. *What a glorious day this was!*

Chapter 10

Mommy came back from her trip to Virginia Beach feeling better than she had since she had gotten sick. She seemed to have more energy and she laughed a lot more. She did have her bad days, but they seemed to happen less and less often. Things seemed to have gotten back to normal, for the most part at least.

I'd had my seventh birthday just a couple of weeks before the school year ended. I was playing outside and had just come back for lunch. I walked up the driveway, not noticing the unfamiliar car parked out in front of our house.

"So, how's the birthday girl?"

"Daddy!"

"Well, so tell me, how old are you now?"

"I'm seven! But today's not my birthday? It was two weeks ago."

"Only two weeks ago? Well that's close enough, isn't it? Or would you rather I take your present back to the store?" he teased.

"You got me a present?"

I beamed as he pulled the package from behind his back. He held it out and I took it. I was so excited! *What a surprise. I didn't expect to get any more presents, not this long after my birthday.* I opened it up and stood there looking at my very own Barbie doll! I felt like my eyes were going to burst out of their sockets. I had wanted a Barbie doll for such a long time. I had asked Mommy for one, but she said she couldn't afford it.

"Oh, thank you, Daddy! How did you know I wanted a Barbie doll?"

"Well, I just figured every seven-year-old girl should have a Barbie doll. Am I right?"

"Oh yes! This is the best present ever!"

After the initial thrill and excitement, I realized that Barbie had only the clothes she was wearing.

"Where's the rest of her clothes?" I asked innocently.

Mommy spoke up quickly. "Look at the lovely dress she has on. Isn't it beautiful?"

Her face turned red and she looked embarrassed. Or was it guilt? I couldn't tell, but she definitely seemed nervous.

"But she's supposed to have a bunch of clothes. And shoes and hats, so I can dress her up," I tried to explain.

"Why, you ungrateful little bitch!" Daddy snapped as he raised his hand to hit me.

Mommy stepped forward, and I ducked.

"Don't, John!"

"I'm sorry, Daddy! I didn't mean it. I really love my Barbie," I lied.

"Why don't you go up to your room, while I talk to your father," Mommy suggested.

That's a great idea. I just wanted to get away from him before he got mad again and hit me.

As I slowly walked toward the stairs, I heard my father say, "Why didn't you tell me I was supposed to get clothes, too? I would never have bought the damn thing if I thought it was going to cost me an arm and a leg. Do you know how much those damn clothes cost? They're more expensive than the clothes she has on!"

I didn't hear my mommy's response. She was whispering, so I couldn't make out the words.

I sat on my bed and stared down at the Barbie doll I had wanted so badly. All my friends had Barbie dolls. I was the only girl in the neighbourhood that didn't have one. And now I did. *But what good is it to have a Barbie, if you can't play dress-up with her? What am I supposed to do with her if I can't dress her up?*

"Joanne, he's gone. Come on down for lunch."

I put my Barbie on the bed and went down to the kitchen.

While I ate my sandwich, my mommy said, "I'll try to get some clothes for your Barbie doll at Christmas. Maybe Santa might even get you some. How does that sound?"

"That sounds good, Mommy. Thank you."

I didn't want my mommy to know that it didn't sound good to me. I knew she was trying to make me feel better and I didn't want to hurt her feelings. It was summertime right now and Christmas was so far away. *What am I supposed to do till then? I wish I didn't even have the Barbie. At least, not until she has some clothes to wear.*

"Why don't you get your Barbie and go out and play. Maybe your friends will let you use some of their Barbie clothes," she said, as I finished my lunch.

"Okay," I said quietly.

I picked up my new doll and went downstairs and out the door. I wandered down the driveway slowly and onto the sidewalk. I looked up the street and saw Maureen and Cathy playing on Maureen's front lawn. I walked across the street and up toward her lawn. They were playing with their Barbie dolls. As I got closer, I saw that Cathy had a whole bunch of clothes and hats and shoes and gloves. When I looked over at Maureen's Barbie clothes, I couldn't believe how many she had! There had to be at least twice as many as Cathy had. I sat down on the lawn.

"Look, I got a Barbie for my birthday! My daddy bought it for me."

"That's great, Joanne! Oh, I love the dress she has on," Cathy was saying.

"Is that the only dress you have?" Maureen accused.

"My daddy didn't realize that she needed a lot of clothes and things. He's going out to get me some and bring them back," I lied.

"Here, you can use some of my things," Cathy offered.

"Thanks, Cathy."

"Can I use some of yours, too, Maureen?" I asked.

"I don't have any to spare. I'm using all of mine," she answered quickly, with a pleased look on her face.

I ignored her and started to undress my Barbie so I could put some of Cathy's things on her. I had just gotten Barbie dressed up in a new outfit when I heard Cathy's mom calling her from across the street.

"Coming, mom," Cathy called back to her.

"I gotta go. We're going to the movies today. I need to get my Barbie clothes back," Cathy said as she started packing up her things.

I undressed my Barbie and helped Cathy pack the rest of her clothes and things.

"Bye, Maureen. Bye Joanne. See ya later," she called, as she ran off the lawn and across the street.

I started to dress my Barbie into her only outfit.

"What are you going to dress her in next?" Maureen asked.

I thought I saw a small grin on her face. "Can't I borrow some of your things?"

"I told you. I don't have any to spare."

"But you have so many outfits."

"It's not my fault you're poor. Why should I give up my things just because you're too poor to have any of your own?"

"I'm not asking to keep them. I just want to use them for now and I'll give them right back."

"I said no! They're mine and I don't want to share them with you. Just because you come from a broken home and are poor doesn't mean I should suffer."

"My house isn't broken," I said, confused.

"No, stupid. Your family is broken, not your house. My mother says that your father left you and your family. And when that happens, they call it a broken home. That's why you're so poor. My mother says—"

"My daddy didn't leave us. Mommy and Daddy just didn't get along anymore."

"Don't be such a baby. Only babies still call their parents *Mommy* and *Daddy*. You're just a poor little baby with a broken home."

I felt the tears welling up in my eyes. I quickly stood up, grabbed the rest of my Barbie outfit and walked out to the sidewalk without saying a word.

"Where are you going?" she asked.

I didn't answer. I couldn't speak. She would have known I was on the verge of crying.

"Spoiled sport. I didn't want to play with you anyway," she huffed.

I walked slowly down the sidewalk and across the street without even checking for cars. I felt so sad. So disappointed and lonely. *So this is what it means to be poor?*

I walked slowly into the house and up to my room. As I closed the door behind me, the tears ran down my face. I opened the closet and shoved my Barbie and her things as far to the back on the floor as I could reach. I never wanted to see her again. I didn't want her to remind me that I was poor. That my family was broken.

I sat there on the edge of the bed, tears flowing down my cheeks. I felt so alone. I thought about what Maureen had said about my family being broken. About being poor. And that made me feel even worse. *It isn't fair. Why do I have to be poor? Being poor is a bad thing. Nobody wants to play with a poor person. Being poor means you can't have all the things you want. It means you can't do all the things you want to do.*

The tears kept flowing. I ran my arm across my eyes and face to wipe them away.

As I wiped the tears away, I thought of William. *They always make me feel better. Maybe they can explain why I am poor.*

I wandered into the bathroom and locked the door.

As I sat on the toilet lid, I called out in my mind. *William, are you here?*

Nothing.

Again, I wiped the tears away. *William.*

Again, nothing.

Close your eyes and take a deep breath, I told myself. When I tried to take a deep breath, I couldn't do it. My nose was all stuffed up. I reached for some toilet paper and blew my nose. I tried again to breathe deeply.

William, where are you?

And then I thought. *You know, don't you, William?*

No response.

You know I'm poor, don't you?

I started to cry again. *That's why you won't come to me, isn't it? Nobody wants to be around poor people. Even you, right?*

Still no response.

But I thought you loved me.

I was sobbing now. I wiped my eyes and blew my nose again. *They aren't coming.* I got up and slowly walked to the door. I unlocked the door and shuffled out to the hallway and bumped into my big brother, Teddy.

"Hey, Jo, what's the matter?"

"Nothing," I cried.

"Come on, Jo. What happened? Tell me."

I sobbed as I told him what had happened with the Barbie and what Maureen had said.

"Don't listen to her, Jo. She doesn't know what she's talking about. She's just a bitch!"

I didn't say anything to him about his swearing.

"Why didn't you just kick her ass in? You shoulda beat the shit out of her!"

I could tell he was getting mad. Not at me. At Maureen. And it made me mad at Maureen, too.

He's right. She was just being mean. Next time she says anything, I'm going to give her a pounding. I felt better.

Then I remembered how nice Cathy had been. She didn't mind letting me use her Barbie outfits. She wasn't mean to me. It was just Maureen! *She's just a mean little witch.* I felt so much better.

"Do you want to go out and play?" he asked.

"With you?" I was thrilled.

"Sure. Let's go see if we can find a bunch of kids and start a game."

Yes, I was definitely feeling a whole lot better. In fact, I was beaming! We rounded up a few kids and started to talk about what game we should play.

"How about Red Rover?" I suggested.

"That's a good idea!" Teddy said.

"Yeah," Brian agreed.

"What's Red Rover?" Timmy asked.

"It's a really fun game, but we need a lot more people to play," I said.

"How do you play it?" he asked.

"I'll explain it once every one is here. So why don't we all split up. That way we have a better chance of finding more people," I suggested.

"Okay. Sounds good. Meet everyone back here." We headed in different directions.

I headed over to Cathy's house to see if she was back from the movies. She was. I told her what we were planning and she said she'd love to play.

"Do you think your brother Paul will want to play?" I asked.

"Oh, I'm sure he will."

"And what about Jimmy and Linda?"

"Probably. I'll ask them."

"Okay, I'll go and find some more kids. You go and ask your brothers and sister and I'll meet you back in front of my house."

I found two more kids before heading back to the meeting place. By the time everyone came back, we had twenty-four kids! *This is going to be great! It's always more fun when there's a lot of players.*

I explained how the game worked. "So, first we pick two captains and they pick who will be on the two teams. Team one will line up down there, side by side. You spread your arms out and hold hands." I pointed in the direction the first team would go and continued with the instructions.

I pointed and said, "Then, team two will line up down there, the same way, with the two teams facing each other. Now let's pick our teams and get in position. I'll explain the rest once we're lined up."

We picked our teams and everyone scrambled to get into the lines. It took a bit of time because not everyone understood what they were supposed to do. Once we were all lined up, I continued to explain how the game works.

"We start with team one. The captain picks a person from team two that you want to call over. The whole team calls out, Red Rover, Red Rover, we call so-and-so over. You call out the name of the person the captain selected. Then that person runs over and tries to break through the line. If the person breaks through the line, they get to pick someone to come back and join their team. If they don't break through, then they have to join the opposite team. Then we switch to the second team and go back and forth until there is only one person left on one of the teams and they're the loser. If no one is left on a team when it's over, then no one loses."

Some of the kids didn't completely understand how it worked, so a bunch of us showed them a practice round.

Teddy and I were both on team two. We'd been playing for quite a while and everyone was having a lot of fun. Team one was down to only two people, Peter and Maureen! It was their turn to call someone over and they called me.

I braced myself and took off running as fast as I could, aiming toward their held hands. I burst through! The fate of the loser was in my hands. I picked Peter to join our team, leaving Maureen as the loser.

Everyone was laughing and fooling around and some of the kids were teasing Maureen because she was the loser. It was all in fun, but I still felt a little sorry for her.

Some of the kids had already run off, laughing and goofing around, when Maureen came running toward me, screaming, "You cheated! I'm not the loser, you are. You're a little witch and you're the loser."

I looked around for Teddy but he had already taken off down the street. "I didn't cheat! You lost, fair and square."

"Did not. You're the loser. And your mom's a loser."

How dare she say something bad about my mom! "You take that back!"

"I won't. Loser, loser, loser," she sang out mockingly.

"I'm warning you! Take it back!"

"My mom says it was a good thing it was your mom who lost her breast. She says that the one she has left is big enough to more than make up for the one they cut off," she shouted out, laughing.

I don't remember what happened next. All I know is that I was suddenly on top of Maureen, pounding her with my fists. And then Teddy was pulling me off of her. I had no idea when he had come back.

"Come on, Jo. Let's go home."

Once we got in the house, we both headed down to the basement. Then Teddy asked me who started the fight.

I told him what had happened and what Maureen had said about Mom.

"Good for you, Jo! She deserved everything you gave her. She's a mean little bitch and her mother is even worse. You stood up for yourself and for Mom. You didn't let her run you down. I'm proud of you, Jo."

I felt so pleased that I had made Teddy proud. But I also felt bad that I had beaten up on Maureen. And I was also still really angry about what she'd said about Mom. It was so confusing to keep bouncing from feeling bad, to feeling good, to feeling bad again.

I looked at Teddy's face and I felt good again.

"I think maybe it's better if you don't tell Mom what that little bitch said about her. Okay?"

"Okay, Teddy. I won't."

And then I heard my mom calling. "Supper's ready!"

"Coming," we both yelled, as we ran up the stairs.

Chapter 11

It was Saturday, and I woke to the sunshine streaming in my bedroom window. I could hear the birds singing in the yard. It was spring and I was excited about the nice weather coming. I lay in my bed thinking over the last several months.

Once the summer was over, we had all settled back into school. I never talked about my Barbie again. In fact, I never played with her again. She was still hidden in the back of the closet. I never got any more outfits for her at Christmas. The truth is, I really didn't think about her at all. During the winter, we spent most of our time outside, playing in the snow. But now, I was looking forward to the change in weather.

I got up and went downstairs for breakfast, and then we all went down to the basement to play. Carol was playing by herself and I was wrestling with my brothers. My little sister Shirley was still up in our room playing on her own.

"Kids, listen. I want you to get dressed and get ready to go out," my mom called out from upstairs.

We stopped fooling around. *I wonder if something's up.* It was too early to go out and play. We usually played in our pyjamas on Saturday mornings, until it was time to go out to play. None of the other kids would be out yet.

"What's up, Ma?" Teddy shouted up the stairs.

"Your father is coming to take you kids out for a while today."

"Yeah, Dad's coming!" we all sang out.

We hadn't seen our father since the summer. This was exciting. *I wonder where he's going to take us.* I ran up the stairs behind Teddy.

Once I was dressed, I went back down to the kitchen. "When's he coming?" I asked.

"He's on his way. He should be here shortly," Mom answered as Teddy walked in the kitchen.

"Can we watch for him in the living room?" I asked. We weren't normally allowed to hang out in the living room. "We'll be good, I promise. We won't make a mess." Kevin and Carol came into the kitchen.

"Well, alright, as long as you just sit quietly and don't make a mess."

Teddy and I ran into the living room.

"Can I go downstairs and play while I'm waiting?" I heard Kevin ask.

"That's fine. Go ahead."

"Me, too?" I heard Carol jump in.

"Just don't get yourselves messed up, you hear?"

"We won't," they said together as they ran down the stairs.

Teddy sat in the chair that faces the front window, so that he would be able to see Dad's car as it pulled up in front of the house. And I sat on the couch, waiting patiently. Well, as patiently as I could.

"He's coming, Ma!"

Teddy jumped out of the chair and ran to the kitchen as I jumped up and ran to the window to look. I could see my dad pulling into the driveway and backing out again to park in front of the house.

"Why don't you go back in the living room, Teddy, until I call you? I want to talk to your father first, before you go," Mom said.

Teddy came back and sat in the chair. I stood at the window, looking out at Dad's car. I had seen him walking up the driveway when Mom was talking to Teddy. I heard the knock at the door.

"What do you mean?" I heard my mom say. "You can't do this. It isn't fair! Don't do this, John," I heard her whispering.

Then the door closed, so I couldn't hear what they were saying. Something was wrong. *What is it? It doesn't make any sense. If he changed his mind, he wouldn't still be here. What's going on?* I went back and sat on the couch. I looked at Teddy's face. He was thinking the same as me. I could tell. He knew something was wrong, too.

I heard the door open and my mom called down the stairs, "Kevin, get your shoes and coat on. Your father's waiting."

Oh, good. Everything's okay after all. But then I realized that my mom sounded strange. *It sounds like she's been crying. Something still isn't right.*

"Teddy, Joanne, Carol, come here."

Oh good. I was wrong. Everything's fine. Teddy and I ran into the kitchen, where my mom was sitting at the table.

"Your dad is only taking Kevin with him today," she said quietly, her voice cracking.

"How come? I don't understand." I asked.

"He wants to go look at new cars and there's too many of you for him to take along."

"But how come Kevin gets to go?"

"You wouldn't enjoy yourself. You would be bored to tears. Going from one dealership to the next. You wouldn't like it."

"Then Kevin won't like it either," I argued.

"Kevin's a boy. Boys don't mind doing things like that."

"But, what about Teddy? He's a boy too. Why isn't Teddy going?"

"Because your father is a mean, selfish bastard and you're better off without him!" my mother cried out though her tears. She got up and ran up the stairs to her room.

I looked at Teddy and he looked back at me. I could see the disappointment and hurt on his face. He walked past me into the living room and sat back down on the chair. I followed him and sat on the couch. Teddy was staring out the window silently and I was staring at Teddy.

How could my dad do this? Why would he do this? What did we do wrong? I kinda understand that he wouldn't want to take us girls. He's going to buy a car and that's a boy thing to do. But why isn't he taking Teddy? That doesn't make any sense at all.

I kept looking at Teddy. I could tell that he was trying hard not to cry. My heart ached for him. As I looked at the disappointment in his face, I held back my tears.

I heard Kevin run up the stairs and out the door. A few seconds later, I heard the car door slam shut and the car drive off.

Teddy sat there staring at the road. And I sat there staring at Teddy.

"I'm sorry you couldn't go, Teddy," I said quietly.

"I didn't want to go anyway," he choked out as he got up from the chair and went upstairs to his room.

Tears filled my eyes and a lump formed in my throat. I stood and slowly walked toward the stairs. I wiped my eyes as I slowly made my way up toward my room. As I got to the top of the stairs, I turned into the bathroom instead.

The tears flowed freely down my face as I closed and locked the door. I pulled some toilet paper off the roll, wiped my face and blew my nose. I sat down on the lid and took a deep breath. With each deep breath, I felt the tears easing. So I closed my eyes and just kept breathing. Slow, deep breaths. As I felt my body relaxing, I heard that familiar voice in my mind.

Good morning, dear little one. We are so pleased to be with you.

Hello, William.

And how are you on this fine, spring morning?

I'm sad. And confused.

Well, which is it?

Which is what?

Are you sad? Or are you confused?

I'm both. I'm sad. And I'm confused.

That is not possible, dear child. You cannot feel two different emotions at the same moment.

But I do! Honest!

Do you think perhaps that you are alternating between feeling sad and feeling confused?

What does alternating *mean?*

Switching back and forth.

Well, I suppose so. Maybe I am switching back and forth.

And which feels better?

Neither. They both feel bad.

But one doesn't feel quite as bad as the other, does it?

I thought about this for a moment. *I guess not.*

So, which one feels better?

I guess it feels better to be confused than to be sad.

Good. Now we're getting somewhere.

We are?

Yes, we are. So, tell me little one, what are you confused about?

I don't understand why my dad only wanted to take my brother Kevin out with him today.

Then I paused and thought. *Is it because he only loves Kevin? It is, isn't it? Why doesn't my dad love the rest of us? What did we do? Is it because we're bad that he doesn't love us?*

No, dear little one. You are not bad. Your father is just lost.

What do you mean, lost?

Your father has lost his way.

I still don't understand.

Your father has lost his ability to love.

But what about Kevin? He still loves Kevin. That's why he took him out and not us, isn't it?

No, dear child. Your father does not have access to the feeling of love. That is what we mean when we say that he is lost.

But, can't you help him? You could show him how to love, couldn't you?

We are, little one.

You are? Then why is he lost?

We can only send our love to him and hope that he feels it and responds to it.

And will he? I want him to be able to love. I want him to love me. And Teddy. All of us.

Do not be concerned about your father's ability to love. Just continue to be filled with the love that you have.

But—

Think about the love you feel for your mother and that she feels for you. Think about the love you feel for your brother and that he feels for you.

I thought about this for a moment and started to feel better. *But I love my father. Why doesn't he love me back?*

What do you think?

He doesn't know how to love me back?

That's right! You've got it. He doesn't know how to love anyone, right now.

Will he learn? Will he start to love me some day?

Yes he will, dear child.

And Teddy, too?

Yes, little one.

When?

That is up to him.

What do you mean?

Your father has his journey through this physical life and you have yours. How he makes this journey is up to him.

But isn't there anything I can do to help?

Yes, there is.

What? What can I do to help?

Keep loving him, no matter what.

But I already do.

Yes, we know you do. Just always remember that your love for anyone should not depend on whether they love you back. Do you understand?

I think so.

Trust us when we say that as long as you send love out, you will always receive love back.

Does that mean that if I send my love out to my dad, then he will send his love back to me?

It means that you will receive love back. It may not come from the same source that you sent it out to. But that should never matter.

But I love my brothers and they love me back. And I love my sisters and they love me back. And I love my mom and she loves me back. How come—

And how do you feel about their love for you?

I thought about my mom. And I thought about my brothers and my sisters. And I thought about my friends. *Wonderful. It feels wonderful. I feel wonderful.*

Yes, we can feel your joy!

I felt the warmth of their love wash over me. And my heart filled with joy and excitement. I felt so grateful to have these wonderful friends in my life.

And I love you, William! I love you so much!

Our love for you is greater than you know.

I stood up, feeling the glow of their love for me and the glow of my love for them. This was going to be a glorious day after all.

Chapter 12

The school year was almost over and I was looking forward to the summer holidays. There were only two weeks left and we would be off for a whole two months! I was going to be turning eight years old in another month, and my girlfriend Cathy was turning eight the next weekend.

When I woke up that morning, I'd been dreaming. I did that a lot. I usually remembered my dreams when I first woke up, but if I didn't run them through my mind right away I would forget them. Or I would remember them later, if something happened that reminded me of the dream.

The dream I'd had that morning was about Cathy. I thought about it for a while so I would remember it later. I wanted to tell Cathy about it when I saw her.

I got up and got dressed right away. It was Sunday morning and I'd slept in later than usual. I wanted to quickly eat my breakfast and get outside to play.

Mom didn't make us porridge on the weekends, so I made myself some toast and jam. I gobbled it up and washed it down with some orange juice. I put the dishes in the sink and ran toward the door.

"I'm going outside," I shouted to no one in particular. I ran down the street to call on Cathy. When she came outside, we stood in her driveway, discussing what we wanted to do. We ended up playing hopscotch for a while and then decided to head down to the creek to hang out.

As we walked down the street, I remembered my dream. "I had a dream about you last night."

"You did? What was it about?"

"It was about your birthday next weekend."

"It was? Tell me more!"

"You were in your living room, unwrapping presents."

"How many presents?"

"A lot. Maybe eight or nine."

"Which was it, eight or nine?" she squealed.

I closed my eyes and saw the dream playing in my head, just like the memory of a real event. I counted the gifts lying on the floor at her feet.

"It was nine."

"What'd I get? What'd I get?"

"You got some clothes. And a skipping rope."

"What else? What else?"

"I don't know. That's when I think the dream ended."

"No it's not! Tell me more. Please! You remember more. Come on. Just think."

She was so excited and happy. I didn't want to disappoint her, but I really didn't think there was any more to the dream. "I really don't remember anything more. I'm sorry, Cathy."

"Just try, Joanne. Please. Close your eyes and try to remember."

So, I closed my eyes. At first, there was nothing, but then all of a sudden I saw pictures flashing through my mind. I wasn't sure if I was just imagining it or whether it was part of the dream.

"What do you see? What do you see? Tell me."

"I see this beautiful, new pink bike, with a big pink ribbon on it."

She squealed! She was so excited. She said she had begged her dad to buy her a new bike for her birthday, but he had told her that he didn't think they were going to be able to get it this year.

I started to worry. I didn't want her believing that the dream was going to come true, if it wasn't. But I couldn't bring myself to say so. She was just so happy. And it felt good to think that I had made her feel so happy.

We met up with a couple of our friends at the creek and played with them until lunchtime and then again after lunch. Cathy was happy all day. I could tell she was still beaming about my dream.

The following Saturday, as we were just finishing up lunch, I heard the knock on the door. "I'll get it," I said and jumped up from the table.

I opened the door and there was Cathy. "Happy Birthday, Cathy!" I sang out.

"You were right! I got it! I just knew I would! Thank you so much!"

"What are you talking about?"

"My bike! I got a bike for my birthday! Just like you said. And look—" She moved to the side of the house and came back, steering her new bike for me to see. And there it was. The exact same bike that I had seen in my dream last week. I couldn't believe it! *How is this possible?*

She was beaming. I had never seen her so happy. I was so thrilled for her. She kept talking as though I was the reason she got the bike. I knew I had nothing to do with it, but I was still amazed that it looked exactly like the one I had described.

"This is exactly how you described it! I just knew I was going to get it! I could feel it. How did you know I was going to get my new bike? How did you know what it was going to look like?"

"I don't know. It was just a dream."

"But you described it exactly. Did my dad show it to you?"

"No, honest. It was just a dream!"

"I love your dreams. They're magic! I gotta go. We're going to the movies for my birthday!" She jumped on her new bike and rode down the driveway.

I closed the door feeling so thrilled for Cathy. I knew how much she wanted a new bike and I was so happy that her dad got it for her, after all. *But how come it looked exactly like the one I had seen in my mind? I should go and ask William. They'll know! They know everything!*

I ran up the stairs and into the bathroom. I closed and locked the door. I put the lid down and sat. I shut my eyes and started to take several slow, deep breaths. It didn't take long for me to feel relaxed and calm.

Hello, luv. And how are you feeling on this glorious day?

William! You're here! I'm so glad you're here!

Of course we're here. We are always here.

I let that one go by. I was too excited. I was just so happy to be talking to William. I wanted to tell them all about my dream. And the bike!

I had a dream last week. I dreamt that my girlfriend Cathy got a beautiful, pink bike for her birthday. It's her birthday today.

Well, actually the bike wasn't even part of my dream. I paused to catch my breath.

Yes, go on.

And she got it! The bike, I mean.

How nice, for her.

No, I mean, the exact bike! The one that I saw in my mind! How did I see her bike in my mind? A whole week before she got it? How did that happen?

How did you feel when you saw the bike in your mind?

I was excited for her. I was happy for her. When I told her my dream, she got so excited and I felt the same excitement for her.

That's right! So we showed you what was waiting for her.

You showed me?

Yes.

How did you show me?

The same way we have shown you everything before.

But, I wasn't in here. I wasn't in the bathroom. How did you show me when I wasn't in here?

Dear, dear child. You do not have to be in this place to have access to us.

I don't? But, I thought—

Dear little one. It doesn't matter where you are. You always have access to us.

I do? Why didn't you tell me before?

We have, dear child. Many times.

You did? Why don't I remember? Why didn't I already know?

You learn when you are ready to learn. You hear our message when you are ready to hear our message.

Does that mean I am stupid?

No, dear little one. There are many that go through their whole physical life without ever knowing.

There are? Then that means I am smart! I was beaming. And then I started to think about what I had just discovered. I couldn't believe it! *This is huge! To think that I can talk to William, whenever I want. Wherever I am at the time. I always thought I had to come to the bathroom to talk to them. This is the most amazing news. This is going to change everything!*

I could barely contain myself. I jumped off the toilet and ran out of the bathroom. *Are you still here?* I asked as I ran down the stairs.

Of course we are, dear child, they answered patiently, amused.

I ran through the kitchen, down the few steps to the door and out into the driveway. *Are you still here?* I asked again.

We are, little one.

I squealed. I ran into the backyard. *Are you still here?* I already knew the answer. I could feel them! That wonderful, familiar feeling of love. Of warmth and comfort. Of pure joy! I wrapped my arms around myself to hold this glorious feeling inside me. *You're here! I can feel you! I am outside and I can still feel you!*

We are, dear little one!

And I felt their joy. My joy. Our joy! I threw my arms out and twirled around, soaking up that glorious feeling! I raised my face to the skies and felt the warmth beaming down. *The warmth of the sun? No. Well, yes, I can feel the warmth of the sun on my face, but it's so much more than that!* I felt the warmth of their love for me. Of my love for them. Of our love for each other. *Oh, William! Thank you so much. Thank you, thank you, thank you! I love you. I love you so, so much!*

Our love for you is greater than you know.

And my heart sang!

Chapter 13

As I slowly woke up, I noticed a strange quiet in the house. There was usually at least one person up before me. But not this morning. I lay in my bed, straining to hear whether there was someone else awake. *Maybe they're just being really quiet.* But I didn't hear anything. So I stretched out my arms and tucked them up under my head, thinking back over the last several months.

It had been a wonderful summer. William had been right. I could now talk to them whenever and wherever I wanted. It wasn't as if they were always around. I mean, they never just showed up as I was walking down the street, for instance. Well, they did come to me then, too, but only when I called out to them. At first, I kept testing them whenever I thought about it. Like if I was just sitting around by myself on the front lawn, I would call out to them in my mind and there they were. It felt so good to know that I could call on them any time I wanted to.

I remember one day I was walking down the street on my way home, staring at the cracks in the sidewalk in kind of a daze. Suddenly I thought of William, so I quickly looked around to make sure no one was near me, before testing out how this would work. Oh I know I don't actually talk out loud with them, but I still didn't want to have someone suddenly show up when I was in the middle of talking to them. I had decided a long time ago that it was so much easier to keep William all to myself. Other people wouldn't understand. Or if they did, they probably wouldn't believe me. And besides, I had a feeling that William agreed with me. So when I didn't see anyone around, I called out to William in my mind.

William. Are you here?

Nothing.

William. Can you hear me?

Hello, little one. And how are you on this fine day?

William! You are here. I can really call on you, whenever I want.

Of course you can.

Oh, William, I am so happy. I wasn't sure if I could do it again.

You need to trust in us. You need to trust in yourself.

I do trust you. But—

But what, dear one?

Well, I just wasn't sure that I could do it.

You need to trust in yourself.

I thought about this for a moment. They were right. It was myself I didn't trust. I wasn't sure I could do it. I trusted them, but not myself. And now that I knew I could call on them no matter where I was, I felt so much better. I felt proud of myself.

We are very pleased that you understand. And we are proud of you, too.

Thank you, William. I sometimes forget you can hear my thinking. Even when I'm thinking to myself.

We are pleased you are coming to realize that we are always with you.

Even when I'm with my friends?

Always.

Even when I am asleep?

Always.

Even when I'm sad? Or scared?

Always.

I thought about this for a moment. I thought about times when I'd been so desperate to talk to them, but couldn't reach them.

But then, why—

You didn't have access to us when you were feeling so bad. But we were still there with you.

But I still don't understand. If you are always here, then why don't I always know it?

Because we always feel only the greatest love for you. And when you are feeling bad, you do not have ready access to the love we are feeling.

But I could feel it now. I could feel that familiar warmth spreading all through my body. That feeling of me loving them. And them loving me. With no real separation between my love for them and theirs for me. It was as if we were one. As if we were all the same person. And just when I thought there was no better feeling in this world, the love and joy and peace and excitement all mixed together washed over me in a feeling so strong there were no words to describe it.

I love you, William. I love you so much.
Our love for you is greater than you know.

And as I felt myself floating in this wonderful feeling, I realized that I had already walked all the way home, totally unaware of anything around me. Except William.

It's like that so much of the time now. And the dreams! I seem to be dreaming so much more than before. And remembering a lot more of my dreams. My friends had come to love my dreams. In fact, they were all starting to call them "magic dreams." So many of the dreams were like the one I had of Cathy. I would tell my friends what I dreamed and within a short period of time, some of the things I had described would actually happen. Oh, I don't mean that all my friends were getting gifts. Sometimes the dreams were about getting something, like a present. But most of the time, I would describe an event, like a little story, and then my friends would tell me later that it actually happened, just as I had described. I'm pretty sure it was because of my dreams that I became more popular. All my friends wanted to hang out with me. I never told them that sometimes I actually added to the original dream the way I had done with Cathy. There were times when the dream was just this little, tiny piece. And then, as I told them the dream and they pushed me to continue, when there wasn't anything more, I would suddenly get little flashes of images or conversations in my mind. The funny thing is, a lot of the things and events that actually came true were those extra parts that came to me as I was telling the dream story.

As I lay there in my bed remembering, I noticed that it was still so quiet in the house. *It must be really early. I don't mind, though. I like thinking back over happy events. It makes me feel good.* So I settled back to thinking about the wonderful summer.

I always had friends to play with because of my increased popularity. We would play hopscotch, skipping rope and, when there were lots of us around, we would organize games to play. But best of all was the swimming. I was a really good, strong swimmer and I just loved it.

There was a swimming pool in the apartment building parking lot, behind the street where I lived. To use the pool, you were supposed to live in one of the two buildings the pool belonged to, but as long as someone from the buildings signed you in, you could use the pool. So almost every day I would meet one of my friends over at the pool. We would wait at the gate for adults to arrive, with our swimsuits on and a towel tucked under our arms. Some days it didn't take long at all to get signed in and other days it took hours. Sometimes, the adults were nice to us, even if they didn't want to sign us in. And then other times, they weren't very nice at all.

One day, Janice and I had been waiting at the pool for about a half hour. Only a few adults had come down to the pool and none of them had been willing to sign us in. As we waited, I looked over at the two buildings, watching for the adults with towels.

"Look," I said to Janice, as I nodded my head toward the closest building.

"What?"

"Here come a couple," I continued, as I anxiously waited for them to get closer.

"Good morning, sir. Good morning, ma'am. Could you sign us in please?" I asked, as they came up to the gate.

"No, sorry. We're only going to be here for a short while."

"That's okay. We don't mind staying for just a short while," I said, as they opened the gate.

"We really don't want the responsibility," he snapped.

"Okay," I said quietly, watching him sign the book.

And so it went for at least another hour. The man and woman who had said they were only going to be there a short while were still in the pool. It was getting hot, and the pool looked so inviting. More and more people came, as the afternoon sun beamed down on us. *The more people, the better chance we have for getting someone to sign us in.*

"I'm getting hot," Janice whined.

"Wait. Look. Here comes someone else."

I stepped forward to greet them. "Good afternoon, miss. I wonder if you could please sign us in."

"Sure. Didn't I see you here yesterday?"

"Oh, thank you, ma'am. This is really nice of you. Thank you so much," I babbled, as she signed herself in the book and then asked our names so she could sign us in.

"We won't be any trouble, miss. Thanks again for signing us in," I went on, as she walked over to find herself a spot to sit.

And so we were finally in for the day! It took me a bit of time, but eventually I got in the pool and the water felt so good. It always took me awhile to get into the water, but once I was in, I usually stayed in for a long time. We swam and swam and laughed and played. It was a wonderful day.

The following day, we got signed in much faster. And the next day, too.

Then one day, we had been waiting for at least two hours and no one seemed to want to sign us in. I was starting to think that maybe we should just give up and go do something else, when I saw a man coming toward the pool. I perked up and got ready to greet him.

"Good afternoon, sir," I said, smiling at him. I yanked at Janice's arm to pull her up beside me.

"Could you sign us in?" I continued, still smiling.

"Where's your parents?" he snapped.

I was instantly on alert. "My mom's at work," I answered honestly.

"What about your father?" he asked angrily.

"My dad doesn't live with us," I said as I tried to figure out why he was asking us these questions. *And why was he so angry?*

"Where do you live?" he demanded.

I hesitated. *Should I lie to him? No, I better not.*

"Just over there, on that street," I answered, pointing.

"Well then, go on home. You don't belong here," he barked.

"But we just want to go swimming. It's so hot today," I said, trying to sound as nice as I could.

"I pay for this pool and you don't. You brats don't belong here. Now get out of here before I get the superintendent to kick you out."

He was really angry and I was scared. "Come on, Janice. Let's go," I said quietly, as I started to walk away. I felt like I was going to cry, but I didn't.

As we were walking away, I heard him shout, "And don't come back. If I see you here again, I'll have you reported."

It was more than a week before we went back. We were too scared that we would run into that horrible man again.

I was still really nervous about the man seeing us, but we finally got up the nerve to go over to the pool again anyway. We had waited until the afternoon to go, hoping he might be gone by that time of the day.

We had just gotten there when I looked over at the building and saw a man and women coming toward us. My heart felt like it was up in my throat. I could feel my face turning red. *Was it him?* And then I relaxed. It wasn't him after all. I was so relieved.

As they got closer, I stepped forward. I smiled and said my usual, "Good afternoon, sir. Good afternoon, ma'am."

"Good afternoon," they both said together.

This seems promising. "Could you sign us in today?" I asked hopefully.

"No, sorry. We really don't feel comfortable being responsible for you," she answered.

"That's okay, ma'am," I responded pleasantly. I didn't want to push it. At least they were being nice to us. "Thank you anyway," I continued, as they opened the gate and walked in.

I was still watching them when I saw the man sign the book. They were whispering and looking over at Janice and me. I suddenly got nervous. *Oh no. What if they report us?* I wasn't exactly sure what that meant, but I knew it wasn't good. *And maybe we'll never be able to come swimming again. Maybe we should leave. Maybe it was too soon to come back.*

I was just turning to suggest to Janice that we should go, when the lady came back out and asked, "Why did you say thank you, even after we told you we wouldn't sign you in?"

I was confused. I wasn't quite sure what she meant.

"You were nice to us," I answered honestly.

Now she looked confused. "What do you mean by that?" she asked.

I thought about that man. "Some people are mean to us when they say no. But you were nice," I explained.

She stared down at me for a moment and then said, "I've changed my mind. We will sign you in after all."

Suddenly everything was better. I felt so happy. I beamed up at her. *That was a great day*. We never did see that mean man again. *Thank goodness!*

As I lay there in my bed remembering, I suddenly became aware of the silence again. The house was quiet and that was unusual by itself. But the silence was everywhere. And that was really strange. It was eerie. Even when everyone in the house was still asleep, there were always some sounds. Sounds from outside. Sounds of car doors opening and closing. Sounds of cars starting. And sounds of car motors running. Normal sounds. Everyday sounds. *There are always sounds*, I thought. *But nothing? There are no sounds at all.* I knew it wasn't the middle of the night. I knew it had to be morning, because I could see the light coming through the sides of the curtains. I lay there listening to the silence. Confused. And then I sat bolt upright in my bed.

I tore back the curtains to confirm my suspicions. *I was right.* I stared out into my backyard at the thick blanket of white. *It had snowed!* It was still snowing. I gazed at the large flakes of snow gently falling to the ground. I couldn't believe my eyes. I was so excited. The first snow of the season. And there was so much of it.

I jumped off the bed, barely able to hold back my excitement. "It snowed!"

"It's snowing." My sisters woke up.

I ran out of my room and shouted again, "It's snowing!"

As I ran downstairs, I heard Mom shout out groggily, "Keep the noise down. I'm trying to get some sleep."

"But it's snowing, Mom."

"I heard you the first time. The whole neighbourhood heard you. Just keep it down. I have a headache."

She has a lot of headaches. I ran into the kitchen and grabbed the big bag of cereal out of the cupboard. Then I got out the milk, a bowl and a spoon. I poured the cereal and milk into the bowl and barely sat down as I shoveled it into my mouth. I hardly even chewed as I shoved another spoonful in. I knew I shouldn't be rushing. Mom would never let me go out this early anyway. But I couldn't help myself.

When I finished eating, I ran into the living room and opened the curtains as I heard someone coming down the stairs.

"Holy cow! Look it all," I squealed, not knowing or caring who I was talking to.

Now that I was looking out the front of the house, I could see more clearly just how much snow had fallen. I saw the neighbour across the street come out of his house and start to shovel his driveway. I looked over at my mom's car in our driveway. I could barely make out the shape of the car. It was buried beneath what looked like at least a foot of snow.

"Holy shit! You weren't kidding," Teddy said as he stood beside me, staring out the window.

"I told you," I said.

"Dammit. Look at all this shit," I heard my mom saying from upstairs.

I wondered why she wasn't happy about the snow.

"Teddy, will you go out and clean off my car and shovel the drive, when you're done breakfast?" she called out.

"Sure, Ma," he yelled back, and he went into the kitchen to eat.

"You too, Kevin," I heard her say.

Everyone was up now.

"Can I go out and help with the driveway?" I asked.

"There aren't enough shovels," she answered, as she came down the stairs.

"Then can I go out in the backyard and play?"

"It's too early. Why don't you go and work on your oral speech? I thought you said you were going to work on it this weekend."

She was right. I'd been looking forward to starting it. This was the first year we were allowed to write our own speech. The last two years, we had to use the speeches the teacher gave us. I'd still enjoyed doing the oral speeches, but it was going to be so much better, now that we could write our own. I loved writing. My teacher said I had a great imagination. I liked writing made-up stories the best. I hadn't decided what I wanted to write about, but I wanted it to be different. I knew that everyone else would pick boring things to write about. But I planned to write about something fun and interesting and different.

And besides, it had snowed. That changed everything. All I could think about now was going out and playing in the snow.

"But it snowed. I didn't know it was going to snow. I'd rather go out and play in the snow."

"Well, it's too early, so you may as well go and work on your speech while you wait."

So I did. Later that morning, I stopped writing and flipped back over the pages in my notebook. I couldn't believe how much I'd written so far. In fact, I was almost finished. I'd been so busy writing I hadn't even noticed how much time had gone by. I quickly got dressed and went downstairs to see where everyone was.

"How did you make out with your speech?" Mom asked as I walked into the kitchen.

"Good. I'm almost finished," I answered, feeling pleased with myself.

"That's good. Now aren't you glad I made you get started?"

"I guess so," I answered, not willing to admit how glad I really was.

"Can I go out and play now?"

"I suppose so. Now listen here, Joanne. I'm taking your brothers to the skate exchange this morning, so don't go far, you hear?"

I instantly perked up. "Can you get me some girls' skates?"

"I'll look, but they never seem to have your size in girls' skates. I may have to get you boys' ones again."

"Please, Mom. I've never had girls' skates. I hate having to wear boys' skates."

"I'm sorry, but you'll just have to be satisfied with whatever they have. Would you rather I didn't get you anything?"

I hung my head and quietly said, "No, I guess not."

But I wasn't sure whether that was true. The other kids always made fun of me when I wore boys' skates. Not my girlfriends. But the boys did. But I loved skating, so I didn't know which was worse: not having skates at all or having to wear boys' skates. I hated having such big feet. That was why they never had any girls' skates for me.

Maybe this year will be different. Maybe an older girl will turn her skates into the exchange.

"So why don't you get your winter things on and go on out? And don't forget. I don't want you going far," she said, as she put on her coat.

"I'm going to call on Cathy and maybe go to the creek, tobogganing. Do you have any boxes I can use?" I asked.

"There's a couple of big ones down in the laundry room. I'll see you in a little while. Bye," she called out as she closed the door behind her.

I got my winter things on, went downstairs and got one of the boxes, and then ran back up and out the door to call on Cathy.

*

When we got to the top of the huge hill at the creek, I started to open up the box to make it flat. There were already quite a few other kids tobogganing. I looked around at them all. Everyone else had real toboggans, including Cathy. *I wish I had a real toboggan*, I thought, as I finished flattening out my box. Cathy had already positioned her sled and was pushing off when I finished and moved over to the edge of the hill. I stood there and watched as she squealed and laughed going down. Then I positioned my flattened box on the edge, took a few steps backward and took a running start at the box. I landed on the box and used my weight to give a hard push off the edge. I sped down the hill at an incredible speed, screaming all the way. I came to a stop just before going over the second edge to the creek below, laughing as I rolled off the box.

"Wow. That was fantastic!" I said, as I got up.

"Holy cow! I thought you were going to go all the way into the creek," Cathy said, laughing at the same time.

"I know. Me too."

I was still laughing too. I grabbed my box and headed back up the hill with Cathy.

I had gone down for the seventh time and was heading back up, when I accidentally stepped on one of the flaps of my box. The box had started to get soggy, so it had become harder to pull up the hill. As my foot caught the flap, I went flying and tumbled back down the hill, knocking the wind out of me. Cathy started to laugh, which got me laughing too.

"Are you okay, Joanne?" she choked out from her laughter.

But I couldn't speak, I was laughing so hard. Once I caught my breath and I wasn't laughing so hard, I looked down at the box and saw that it was ripped in two. I didn't think it would make it down the hill another time. I got up and told Cathy I was going to go home and get the other box.

"I'd better go home, too," she said, grabbing her sled. "It's probably lunchtime, so I have to go home and eat," she continued as we headed up the hill.

"See ya after lunch," she called out, as she ran up her driveway.

"Okay, see ya," I called back.

I was deep in thought, walking the rest of the way home, when I looked up and saw my mom's car pulling into our driveway. I started to run, anxious to see if I'd got my first set of girls' skates.

I reached the driveway just as they were getting out of the car.

"Did you get my skates?" I asked, as I slipped on a patch of snow. My brothers burst out laughing and I started to laugh too, as I got up from the ground.

"We did," my mom answered and then handed me the package.

I pulled the package open as my mom warned, "Careful with that."

Then the skates fell out onto the driveway. As I stared down at the skates, my heart sank. They were boys' skates. I couldn't believe it. *Not again*. I was so disappointed. I picked up the skates and slowly walked to the house, the tears flowing silently down my cheek.

I didn't go back to the hill with Cathy that day. I didn't feel like it. I put my new skates away and tried hard not to think about them. And eventually, I did stop thinking about how disappointed I was.

It was several weeks later before I was forced to think about the skates again. It was a Saturday morning and I was practicing my oral speech, when the doorbell rang. Kevin called out that it was for me.

"Coming," I shouted, as I ran down the stairs from my bedroom, through the kitchen and down to the door. It was my friend Diana.

"Hi, Diana!"

"Hey, Joanne. A bunch of us are going down to the school, skating. Pauline says they finished making the rink last night. Wanna come?"

I hesitated. I thought about my skates. I wasn't sure if I wanted anyone to see that I still had boys' skates.

"I don't know," I started slowly.

"Oh come on. It'll be fun. Everybody's going to be there," she urged.

That's what I'm afraid of. But my love for skating won. *After all, I can't go all winter without skating, can I? Of course not.* I had to just accept the fact that I was stuck with boys' skates for another whole year.

"Okay, just give me a minute to get ready. Come on in."

When we got to the school, I saw that Diana was right. Everybody was there. I couldn't believe how many people there were! We went over and sat on one of the wooden benches that had been placed around the sides of the rink.

I pulled one of my skates out of the bag and put it on the ground. I took off my boot and started to open up the laces on my skate. As I bent over to put my foot in the skate, I caught a glimpse of Diana's skate out of the corner of my eye. I tried not to look at it. I didn't want to draw attention to mine, so I just concentrated on shoving my foot into the first skate. Then I took out the other one and did the same. Once they were both on my feet, I leaned down to start tightening them. As I started to pull on the laces that were closest to my toes, my eyes caught Diana's skates again. This time I couldn't help myself. I shifted my eyes over to her skates without moving my head. They were so beautiful. I could tell they were brand new. They were so white and shiny and they almost sparkled as the sun shone down on them. I felt as though my heart had just dropped into my belly. My throat swelled and tears sprang into my eyes. I quickly looked away and continued tightening my laces.

I hadn't always hated having boys' skates. In fact, there was a time not that long ago when I actually liked it. My mom always said that I was a tomboy because I liked so many boys' things. Like wrestling with my brothers and playing all kinds of sports. And because I preferred to hang around with my brothers and their friends instead of my sister Carol. During that time, I started to think I would rather be a boy. So when I had boys' skates, it was okay, because then I could pretend I was a boy. *But that was then. I'm older now and I don't want to be a boy anymore. I want to be a girl. I want to look like a girl and dress like a girl and do things girls like to do.*

I continued pulling on the laces but I just couldn't seem to get them tight enough. That was another problem with boys' skates. They fit my feet okay, but the ankles were always too big. My feet might be too big, but my ankles were skinny.

"You ready?" Diana asked as she stood up and stepped onto the ice.

"Almost. Just a sec," I answered as I tied the second bow into a knot.

As I stood up, Pauline and Cathy came skating toward us. Then Janice glided up to us and plowed into Pauline. We all started to laugh and for a time, I forgot about my skates. Then Pauline glided away and did a spin and a jump. We all stood there admiring her ability. She'd been taking skating lessons for the last three years and you could really tell. She was so graceful. And she could do so many things we couldn't do, like skating backwards. I wanted so badly to be able to skate backwards. As we all skated along together, laughing and talking, Pauline faced us and skated backwards the whole time. Finally I blurted out, "How do you do that? Can you teach us?"

"Sure." She stopped and we all plowed into her. Janice wiped out and almost pulled me down with her. And we all laughed again.

Pauline showed us how to skate backwards by slowing down her movements so we could see what she was doing. And then we all tried it. At first, we spent most of the time falling down, but then I started to get the hang of it.

"That's good, Jo. You've got it," Pauline shouted. "Now just try to speed it up a bit."

But every time I tried to speed up, I ended up falling. So I slowed down again to get the movement right. I kept trying and trying.

Then all of a sudden Pauline shouted out, "Look it. You're doing it!"

And the second I realized I was really skating backwards, I fell. I didn't care, though. I was so thrilled. All that mattered was that I could now skate backwards.

I got up and did it again and again. The only problem now was that I didn't know how to stop. So Pauline showed me how, and I practiced that too.

I'd been skating nonstop for hours, when I finally skated over to the bench to take a break. The others had stopped for a rest several times before, so they didn't come with me this time. I was sitting on the bench watching my friends skate, admiring Pauline's smooth, graceful movements, when I suddenly heard laughter coming from behind me. I turned around and saw a group of boys from my class.

"Hey, Joanne. What's with the boys' skates?" Wayne called out, laughing. The others were all laughing at me, too.

"Shut up," I shouted back.

"You must be a boy if you're wearing boys' skates," he said. And the laughter continued.

"I am not a boy!" I said, feeling my face turning red.

Then they all started singing out, "Joanne is a boy. Joanne is a boy."

I quickly turned my head away from them so they couldn't see the tears. They continued to make fun of me, and I decided to take off my skates as fast as I could. *I need to get away from here. I need to go home.* I fumbled with the knot on my other skate, trying frantically to get it undone. The tears kept flowing; I couldn't make them stop.

As I got the knot free and loosened the laces, I heard a familiar voice warning, "Knock it off!" It was Teddy.

"Sorry, Ted. We were just messin' around. We didn't mean it," they all chimed in.

I could hear the fear in their voices. Teddy was a lot bigger than they were, and a lot stronger. I felt so proud that he'd stood up for me. I was glad they were scared of him. *It served them right!*

"Hey, Jo. Do you want me to beat them up for you?" Teddy asked as he shook a fist at them.

"No, it's okay. I just want them to leave me alone."

"Get lost or I'll kick the shit outta ya, you hear?" Teddy snapped at them. "And if you bug my sister again, you'll get it," he shouted out, as they all ran away.

"Thanks, Teddy," I said and wiped the tears from my cheeks.

"You okay?" he asked.

"Yeah, I'm okay. I just wanna go home."

"You sure you're okay?"

"Yeah, I was going to go and get some lunch anyway," I could tell he didn't believe me, but he didn't push it.

"Thanks again, Teddy," I said as I picked up my bag and headed toward home.

I didn't even bother to say goodbye to my friends; I just wanted to be alone. As I walked along the sidewalk, my eyes filled with tears again. I reached in my pocket and pulled out a wad of toilet paper, and wiped my cheeks and my upper lip as the tears kept flowing. I couldn't stop them. I slowed down and blew my nose and then sped up again, running the rest of the way.

I had finally stopped crying by the time I got home. I made myself a sandwich for lunch and went out into the backyard. My brothers had made an ice rink in our yard, so I decided I'd rather skate by myself for the rest of the day.

I took my time putting my skates on, trying to make them as tight as possible. There was no hurry. No one was waiting for me. When I pushed off onto the rink, I started to feel better. I loved the way my feet glided on the ice. It made me feel like I was graceful.

Good afternoon, little one. And how are you on this fine day?

William! It's you. I'm so glad you're here.

And we are pleased as well, little one. Once again, we ask, how are you on this fine day?

I'm better now. And then I thought. *Why can't I have girls' skates, like everyone else?*

You can, dear child.

But I can't. My mom says my feet are too big. There are never any girls' skates my size at the skate exchange.

Your feet are not too big. They are just the right size for you. They are the perfect size.

I didn't agree with them, but I didn't want to talk about my feet. *You said I could have girls' skates. How can I?*

Do you trust us, dear one?

Of course I do.

Then close your eyes.

So I did.

Now visualize yourself wearing a beautiful pair of girls' skates.

I pictured myself looking down at the most beautiful pair of white, shiny skates. Just like Diana's.

That's very good. Now feel yourself skating in those skates.

In my mind, I could feel myself gliding across the ice. The skates fit me perfectly and I could feel that I was as graceful as a swan. In fact, I was as graceful as Pauline. Then I felt myself spinning on the ice, and the feeling was exhilarating. I took off again, soaring across the ice at a speed I had never gone before. I could feel the cool air brushing against my face as I smoothly cut the corners of the rink and glided back down the other side. I was skating at an incredible pace, my arms outstretched, giving me balance and grace. I could hear the blades of the skates cutting through the ice and I could feel my ankles holding sturdily, with a firm comfortable fit. As I rounded the corner again, my arms still outstretched, I felt so alive. So free. I felt like I could do anything. And when I came around the corner again, for what felt like the twentieth time, I turned in toward the centre of the rink, pulled my arms into my body tight and started another spin. I was spinning faster and faster until I started to feel dizzy. So I slowed down again, putting my arms back out to help balance myself. As I ended the spin, I raised my face up to the sky, feeling so full of joy.

We feel your exhilaration. Your joy. We are very pleased.

As I heard William in my mind, I suddenly realized that it hadn't been real after all. *But it had felt so real.* I felt disappointed and confused.

But it wasn't real.

Of course it was.

No it wasn't. Look it. Look at my skates. They're still boys' skates. It wasn't real at all.

How did you feel when you were skating just now?

Wonderful.

That's right.

But it wasn't real.

Did it feel real?

I thought about how wonderful and how real it had felt. And I could feel the glow of the memory. *Yes, it did feel real at the time. But it wasn't.*

While you were experiencing it, it was real. If it feels real, then it is real.

What do you mean?

How you are feeling at any given moment is all that matters.

But I still don't have girls' skates. Even if it felt like I did, I know now that I still don't.

Tell us, dear child, why do you want these girls' skates?

Because all my friends have them. And because I will skate much better with them. And because it will make me feel happy to have girls' skates. And then I thought about the boys. *And because the boys won't make fun of me*, I added quietly in my mind.

Tell us. How did it feel when the boys were teasing you?

Bad. It felt really bad.

So do you agree that the reason you want these skates is to feel happy?

Yes. Of course.

And how did you feel when you imagined wearing those skates?

Happy. Really, really happy.

We can feel you are beginning to understand.

I think I do. But—

Yes?

But that was just this one time. I don't really have the skates. So I can't just take them with me tomorrow, if I go back to the big rink with my friends.

Of course you can. You can take them with you whenever you want. Just imagine that you have them and you will have them. Truly believe it—truly feel it—and it will be so.

I was starting to get confused again. *Do you mean I will really have them? Or just pretend have them?*

It doesn't matter. It can't matter. And when it really doesn't matter to you, then it will be real.

Are you saying that if I pretend and I really believe my pretending, I will finally get the real ones?

We are.

I suddenly got so excited. *I could do this!* I had just done it before, and I could do it again. So if I just kept doing it—just kept pretending—then eventually I would finally get my girls' skates. I could feel the warmth of William, starting to fill me up with joy. With love. With gratitude.

Oh, William. Thank you so much. I love you.

Our love for you is greater than you know.

Then, as I stepped carefully off the rink, still feeling the warm glow of their love, I noticed that it was already starting to get dark. I suddenly realized that I had spent the whole afternoon with William and my new skates.

What a wonderful day it had turned out to be after all.

Chapter 14

It was early January and the day had finally arrived. My class was doing our oral speeches. Four of my classmates had already done theirs, and Brad was just getting up to do his. So far, they had all been really boring, just as I had expected they would be. *This is great.* I felt really good about mine. It was fun and interesting and even funny. I was pretty sure all the kids would really enjoy it. I had practiced and practiced until I knew it off by heart. Brad started his speech and then suddenly there was silence. *Oh no—he forgot what comes next!*

"It's alright, Bradley. Just take your time," my teacher said.

Some of the kids started to giggle. And I giggled a little myself. But then I started to feel embarrassed. It was as if it was me up there. I could see his face turning red, and it looked like he was going to cry. I felt ashamed that I had joined in with the rest of the class. I couldn't bear to watch him standing there in silence, struggling to remember the next part of his speech. I looked down at my desk and closed my eyes. *You can do it Brad. Just take a deep breath and it will all come back to you.* And then I had another thought.

William. Please help Brad remember.

And in that very instant, Brad continued with the rest of his speech. In fact, it wasn't too bad. It was still pretty boring, but he did a really good job of saying it. By the time he finished, everyone had begun quietly listening. And when it was over, we all clapped for him.

"That was very good, Bradley," my teacher said as he quickly escaped back to his desk.

By the time our afternoon recess arrived, we were all getting tired of listening to speeches about planets and chipmunks and bears and all sorts of other animals. When we all filed back into the classroom afterward, it looked like I wasn't going to get to do my speech that day. The teacher had said it would take two days to get through all the speeches, but I didn't really want to wait until the next day. So I was thrilled when I was the second person she called up after recess.

I got up from my desk feeling excited. And then I was terrified. *Oh no. What if I forget my words, like Brad did?* But then I remembered. William was here. William would help me. And I suddenly felt this incredible calm wash over me. It was as if I was in a dream.

I turned to face the class and started to talk. And talk and talk. And then I realized that everyone was laughing. They were laughing really, really loud. But that was okay. They were supposed to. My speech was supposed to be funny. I had written it to be like a one-person play, with lots of adventure and funny situations. And then, before I knew it, I was finished. And for a moment, I stood there and felt this incredible silence. I could barely breathe.

But then the class was standing up, clapping and cheering and laughing. And when I looked over at my teacher, I saw her clapping and laughing too. I felt so pleased. So proud of myself. *It must have gone well.* I could barely remember actually giving my speech. It was all a blur. And as I walked back to my desk, feeling like I was the happiest kid in the world, I thanked William in my mind.

A few days later, I found out that our teacher had chosen me to do my speech in front of the whole school. Only one kid from each class was chosen, so this was a really big thing. She told me it wasn't going to happen for at least a month.

*

I was excited about the speeches, but I couldn't think about that. I had a serious problem to figure out. Everyone else had already finished dinner and I was staring down at what looked like a mountain of canned peas on my plate. *Yuk!* Teddy and Kevin had both been in a hurry tonight, because their friends were waiting outside for them to finish up. That meant that I couldn't trade anything with them, and Carol didn't want my peas either. So I didn't have any choice. I was going to have to use my water trick.

I got up from the table and started to fill a huge glass with water.

"What are you doing?" Mom demanded.

I jerked and spilled some of the water.

"I'm just getting some water."

"Have you finished your dinner?"

"Not yet, but I was thirsty."

"Don't you be filling up on water. I want you to eat all your dinner and I don't want any excuses, you hear?

"I will. I'm almost done."

I sat back down and stared at the water and the peas. I took a deep breath and braced myself. Then I scooped up a big forkful of peas and shoved them in my mouth. Then, without chewing, I took a big gulp of water and swallowed them whole. I had to be careful though. If I accidentally chewed some, the taste would be all over my tongue. It was going well until the third fork full, when I started to gag and choke. I quickly grabbed a tissue, holding my breath and trying hard not to let the peas touch my tongue. I spit them into the paper and rolled it up in a ball. *Now what am I going to do?* I stared down at the wad of paper. I knew I couldn't just throw it in the garbage. I had tried that before and my mom caught me. After that, she would check if she saw me put anything in the garbage during dinner. I couldn't put it in my pocket, either. I had done that before too. And yes, I got caught.

I looked around frantically. I needed to find a place to hide it, just for a little while. I could come back later and throw it away. And then I saw it! I looked down under the table at the hole in the floor. The stove used to be where the table was now and when it got moved, it left this hole in the floor. It was hidden under the table, so Mom said there was no need to get it fixed. I knew the hole went down to the basement, so I could run down and get it and throw it away down there. Mom would never know. I quickly opened the tissue and shoved the rest of the peas from my plate into it. I figured that if I was going to put them down the hole, I might as well get rid of all of them. I rolled the tissue back up as tight as I could, to make it small enough to fit through the hole. And then I listened to make sure that Mom was still busy reading the newspaper.

I quietly bent over and shoved it down the hole. It was a tight squeeze at first, but then it was gone. As I sat back up, I whacked my head on the table, making a huge thump.

"What the hell are you doing?"

"Nothing. I was just getting up to put my plate in the sink," I answered quickly.

My mom was up and in the kitchen in a split second.

"Have you eaten everything?"

"Yup. See?" I said, holding the empty plate out to show her.

"What's in your pockets?" she demanded.

"Nothing. Look."

I put the plate on the counter and patted my pockets, so she could see that there wasn't anything in them.

"Alright, then. Get started on the dishes."

"But it's Carol's turn."

"Okay, send her up then."

"Okay."

Phew, I thought, as I ran down the stairs to the basement, shouting for Carol to go and do the dishes.

I went straight into the laundry room to look for my wrapped up peas. I searched all over but they weren't there! I didn't understand. I knew that the kitchen was right over the laundry room, so they had to be there. But they weren't. They were nowhere. I started to panic. *I have to find them. If Mom finds them before me, I'll be in huge trouble.* I didn't want to think about what she'd do if she found out. So I kept searching and searching. When I had looked everywhere they could possibly be with no luck, I finally decided that if I couldn't find them, nobody could.

And I was right. Well, sort of. It would be years before they were found. Along with the many others that I sent off to nowhere land. But I did it only when I had no other choice.

A little later that night, I was heading up the stairs to my room when I heard a knock on the door. I was already halfway up the stairs, so I didn't bother to go back down to get it. I knew that Carol or my mom would answer it and besides, it wouldn't be for me at this time of night. As I got to the top of the stairs, I could hear Carol talking. She sounded really excited, so I went back down to see what was up.

"Look, I'm going to a birthday party," Carol squealed, holding the invitation out for me to see.

"When?"

"This Saturday."

"Who's birthday?" I asked.

"Maureen's."

"Maureen's? Where's mine?"

"You didn't get one."

"But—?"

And then my mom spoke up. "Of course she did, Caroline. The invitation is for both of you."

"But it's only addressed to me," Carol argued.

"Joanne is a closer friend with Maureen than you are. They obviously meant to invite both of you. They just made a mistake on the card."

"But—"

"I am not going to argue with you. If Joanne isn't going, then you're not going."

"But that's not fair," Carol whined.

"Alright, that's it. Neither of you are going."

"No, Mom. I'm sorry. Joanne can come."

"You're damn right, she can go. Now go get ready for bed, the both of you."

I never thought any more about the mistake on the invitation. It didn't even occur to me to ask Maureen about it. After all, my mom was right. Maureen was in my class at school. We hung around all the same kids. If anything, it was a little strange that she had invited Carol. My sister didn't even have the same friends as us.

When Saturday finally arrived, we were both so excited. We got our party clothes on way ahead of time and then were forced to just sit around and wait. Mom didn't want us to ruin our dresses. When it was time to leave, we fought over who was going to carry the birthday gift. I won. Mom said that she had spent extra money on the present, because it was from both of us.

Maureen's brother Sam answered the door and let us in.

"Take your boots off here and go on down the stairs. I'll take the gift."

As we came around the corner into the rec room, I saw that most of my friends were already there. Everyone was talking and laughing and playing, so we joined in. We were all having so much fun and making a lot of noise, so I didn't pay much attention when someone spoke up a little louder. And then I heard it again.

"What are you doing here?" Maureen's mom demanded.

Everybody was suddenly quiet. I turned around to see what was happening, when I saw her mom standing at the door of the rec room, hands on her hips, and glaring at me!

"It's okay, Mom. We're all having fun," Maureen spoke up nervously.

"It is not okay. You weren't invited, Joanne. You're going to have to leave. The party is about to start."

"But Mom, please."

I looked around the room and stared into the faces of my friends. Some looked scared. Some looked nervous. And others looked embarrassed. And they were all either staring back at me or trying hard to look away.

"Now get your things on and go home."

"But my mom said I was invited."

"Well your mother was wrong. Now get going, you hear."

"But please, can't I stay? I'll behave, honest."

"No, you can't. You're not wanted here. Don't you understand?"

I didn't answer. I hung my head down and walked toward the pile of coats. Tears filled my eyes. I kept my back to my friends, so they couldn't see. As I put on my coat and headed for the stairs, I heard Carol come out of the bathroom.

"Where are you going, Joanne? What's up?"

And then I heard whispering. I couldn't hear what they were saying, but I didn't need to. I knew. I went up the stairs slowly, hoping, praying that Maureen's mom would change her mind. But she didn't.

As I opened the door to leave, I heard Sam call out, "Hey, Jo, where are you going? What happened?"

But I didn't answer him. I couldn't speak. I knew if I tried to talk, he would be able to tell I was crying. I could feel the tears flowing freely down my cheeks and, by the time I reached my house, I was sobbing uncontrollably.

I was barely inside the door, when my mom shouted out, "What are you doing home? What happened?"

"Mrs. Brent sent me home," I sobbed.

"What do you mean? What did you do?"

"Nothing, honest. She said I wasn't invited," I answered, still barely able to speak through my sobs.

"That horrible woman. How dare she. She's not going to get away with this," my mom shouted, and she stormed over to the phone.

I took off my coat and boots and went up the stairs to the kitchen to listen to my mom on the phone.

"How could you be so mean? And why wouldn't you invite Joanne in the first place?"

And then there was silence as Maureen's mom spoke.

"Well that's ridiculous. They're both in the same class. Carol doesn't even play with her."

Then more silence.

"Well then, you can just send Carol home. And I want the gift back. That gift was from the both of them," she screamed into the phone.

"No, Mom, please. Don't make Carol come home. Please."

My mom paused and stared down at me.

"Please," I sobbed.

It wasn't fair. I couldn't bear the thought of spoiling it for Carol. "Please, Mom."

My mom turned her back to me and spoke into the phone again. "How could you be so cruel? They are only young children."

My mom was no longer yelling, but I could hear a scary tone in her voice. It sounded like pure hatred. I had never heard her sound that way before.

There was silence again as Maureen's mom talked.

"And you better be nice to her. I'm warning you," my mom threatened as she hung up the phone.

"Get your coat and boots on. You're going back over to the party."

But I didn't want to go anymore. *How can I go back there, when they don't want me? What if Maureen's mom is mean to me again? What if she makes all my friends hate me? How can I face them after the way she treated me?*

My mom could see I was hesitating. "Go on, now. It's okay. She said you could go back."

When I arrived back at the party, everyone was happy to see me. Maureen's mom was nowhere around, so I was able to quickly put the earlier experience out of my mind. We played pin the tail on the donkey and laughed, and I had a great time.

It was quite a while later when Maureen's mom called down to say that lunch was almost ready. I suddenly realized I was really hungry. We'd been having so much fun that I didn't notice my hunger creep up on me. I knew that the food was going to be so yummy. It was always really good at birthday parties. And the cake. We would be having cake after lunch. *Mmm.* I couldn't wait.

As Maureen's mom walked in the rec room with a big huge platter, I could smell the hotdogs. *Oh great, my favourite.* I love hotdogs and my mom doesn't let us have them very often. She says they aren't nutritious. But who cares? They're delicious; that's all that matters.

We were all jumping up and down, clapping are hands, as she laid the tray down on the fold-up table.

"Okay, Joanne. It's time to go," she sang out.

"What do you mean?" I asked.

I looked up at her and saw a strange smirk on her face. I didn't understand. *Why is she sending me home again? What did I do?*

"I told your mother that we didn't have enough food for you. Didn't she tell you? I thought she understood that you could only stay until we were ready to eat," she explained politely. But I could hear something else in her voice. She sounded pleased. This didn't make any sense.

"Away you go. I don't want the food getting cold. Come on, everyone. Grab a plate and a hotdog," she said, as she turned her back to me.

I couldn't believe this was happening again. *Why does she hate me so much? What did I do to make her mad?* This time I didn't try to talk her into letting me stay. I went over and got my coat and, without saying a word, I left.

As I opened our door and stepped into the house, I heard my mom call out, "How was the party? Did you girls have fun?"

She walked into the kitchen and froze.

"What happened? Where's your sister?" she demanded.

But I couldn't speak. The tears were pouring down my face and when I looked up at my mom, I could see that her eyes were starting to fill up with tears, too. Then I started to sob and ran to her. I told her what happened, as she held me in her arms.

"That cruel bitch. I want your sister home right now," she blurted out as she grabbed the phone.

"No, Mom, please. Don't spoil it for Carol," I cried out.

"I'm sorry, Joanne. I'm sorry that she treated you this way. That woman is evil. She should never have done this."

I didn't say anything. When I finally stopped crying, I pulled away from my mom's arms and slowly walked out of the kitchen toward the stairs. Once I got to my room, I closed the door and crawled into bed. And the tears came again. I couldn't make them stop.

Why did she do this to me? Why? I cried myself to sleep.

When I woke up, I noticed it was already getting dark. I was still feeling groggy as I snuggled under my covers, feeling relaxed and cozy.

Hello, precious one. And how are you on this fine day?

William! I'm glad you're here. How are you?

We are always well. And how are you, dear little one?

I'm okay. And then I remembered. As I lay there in my bed, I suddenly remembered about the day I'd had. I thought about the party. And Maureen's mean mom. And the horrible way she treated me. *I'm not okay. I feel bad. Really, really bad.*

And why is that, dear little one?

Maureen's mom hates me. And she was really mean to me today. She wouldn't let me stay at the birthday party.

But dear child. You mustn't feel this way. We are so proud of you.

You're proud of me? I don't understand. Why?

You were wonderful today.

I was? How? What do you mean?

Do you recall when you were feeling so rejected?

How could I forget?

That's just it. You did.

I did what?

You forgot. You were able to put the bad feelings aside and have a wonderful time.

I don't know what you're talking about. What do you mean?

Do you remember what happened when you arrived at the party the second time?

Yes, I think so. Well, no, I don't know what you mean.

You were able to put your bad feelings behind you. You chose to feel happy. And you were happy.

But then Mrs. Brent sent me home again. And I felt horrible. Why does she hate me so much? What did I do wrong?

Nothing, dear child.

Then how come she was so mean to me?

Let us ask you something. How did you feel about this lady before today? Before this experience?

I don't know. And then I thought about it for a moment. *I didn't really like her very much*, I admitted.

And why is that, do you suppose?

She's not really very nice to me. Ever.

Is it only you she is, as you say, not very nice to?

Not really. She's kind of nasty to all us kids.

So what does that mean to you?

It means that she is not a nice person.

Do you suppose that she is a happy person?

I don't know. And then I thought about how pleased she seemed when she was sending me home. *I think she is a mean person. And I think it makes her happy to be mean to people.*

Tell us, precious one. Have you ever been mean to someone before?

I blushed. I guess so, I admitted.

And how did you feel at the time?

Angry.

And does angry feel good or bad?

Bad.

So tell us now. Do you still believe she is a happy person?

I thought about the times I felt angry. I thought about the times I'd been mean to someone. And I thought about Maureen's mom. *I guess not. But why is she mad at me? What did I do to her?*

Nothing, dear child. People do not always express their anger or unhappiness at the person they believe is the source of their bad feelings.

As I thought about what William had just said, I realized they were right. There were lots of times that I would lash out at my brothers or sister when I was really mad at my mom. And then I thought about Maureen's mom again. *But why was she only mean to me? Why wasn't she mean to everyone else?*

That is a lesson for another day.

But—

Tell us, child. Do you still believe you did something wrong?

I guess not.

You are absolutely correct. You are a beautiful, loving little girl. You are such a precious child and we are so proud of you.

I could feel their pride for me. I felt that familiar warmth of their love washing over me, filling me up inside. And all that mattered to me was how much William loved me and how much I loved them.

I can feel your love for me. Can you feel my love for you?

Indeed we can. You bring us such joy, little one.

I love you so much William!

Our love for you is greater than you know.

Chapter 15

I woke up feeling refreshed and happy, with no idea how horribly the day would end. And as I lay there in bed, thinking over the past two years, it didn't occur to me that if I'd only known, I might have done things differently. Maybe it didn't have to happen the way it did.

Then I thought about the day I came on my period for the first time. I wasn't confused or even scared. I was excited and a little nervous, but not scared. My older sister Carol had started her period about six months earlier, so my mom had given us both a lesson on what it was all about and what we needed to do to take care of ourselves. She had shown us the supplies we'd need, where she kept them, how to use them and how to dispose of them. But I was still nervous. Not about actually coming on my period, but more about how to tell my mom. She always made such a big deal about these kinds of things. And there was no such thing as a secret in our house. I realized I didn't want my brothers to know about it. I wasn't exactly sure why. I just knew I would be embarrassed. But I also knew I had to tell her.

So I told Carol. I knew she could never keep a secret and I was right. Sure enough, later that morning, my mom called me into her room and told me that Carol had said I'd come on my period.

"Is it true?" she asked.

"Tattletale," I scolded and glared at Carol.

"She was right to tell me. You can't keep this kind of thing a secret. And you shouldn't be embarrassed. This is a normal occurrence. It happens to all girls eventually. I have to admit, though, you are a little young."

"Hey, Jo, I hear you're all grown up," Kevin said as he snickered.

I could feel my face burning with embarrassment.

"You leave her be. Now go on. Get out of here. I want to talk to your sisters."

Here we go. Now I have to endure "the talk." "There's nothing to talk about. I know all about having a period. I already took care of everything."

"That's good. But you need to know that things are going to be different from now on."

I was suddenly on alert. *What does she mean, different? Is there something I don't know about coming on my period? Something she didn't tell me when Carol came on hers?*

"What do you mean, different?"

"Well, you're going to start feeling different. You're going to start developing into a woman."

"Mom." I pleaded for her to stop. I was so embarrassed.

"No. You need to hear this."

"But, Mom!"

"Now listen. This is important. Once you start to develop, boys are going to start showing an interest in you."

"Mom, I don't need to know this!"

"Yes, you do, Joanne. You need to know that you can't just fool around with boys the way you may have in the past. This is very important. You hear?"

"I don't fool around with boys, Mom."

"Well, boys are going to want to. For instance, you might be just kissing innocently. But kissing will lead to other things. And you are going to have to be the strong one. You are going to have to be the one to stop them before you go too far."

I couldn't believe she was saying all this. Was she crazy? "But, Mom!"

"No. I'm not finished. You have to listen to me. If the fooling around goes too far, now that you have your period, you could get pregnant. So it's important that you use all your strength to resist."

I was mortified. "But, Mom, I'm only nine!"

Now my mom looked embarrassed. "Well, yes, I realize that. I'm just saying that you need to be aware, for some time in the future. You just need to be more careful now. That's all I'm saying."

"Sure, Mom. Can I go now?"

"Yes, you can go." She sounded relieved, but she could not have been more relieved than me.

As I thought back on that day, I chuckled. I couldn't believe my mother had said those things to me. I didn't even like boys that way then. In fact, I was only just now starting to like the idea of kissing a boy. And then I thought about my big brother Kevin's best friend, James, and I sighed.

Suddenly I was distracted by my mom's voice in the hallway. "So can you watch the rest of the kids while I'm away?" she was saying.

"Sure Ma. I can do that. What should I make for supper?" Teddy was asking.

"I'll take some spaghetti sauce out of the freezer for you. Now I don't want you letting the girls stay up too late tonight, you hear?"

"No, Ma. I won't."

"And no parties, either. Promise?"

"I promise, Ma. Don't worry. I'll take care of everything."

It was obvious my mom was going away overnight tonight. That wasn't unusual anymore. But the last time it happened, Teddy and Kevin had a big party and invited all their friends over. The house had been packed! Then, when Mom got home the next day and saw all the mess they left, she flipped out. She was so mad they got grounded for two weeks, even after getting the belt.

I was in no rush to get out of bed, so I settled back in and thought some more about the last little while.

It turned out that William had been right about my skates. Every time I went to the rink to skate with my friends, I imagined that I had on a beautiful pair of girls' white skates. And when I went out on the ice, I pretended to skate just the way I had on that wonderful day with William. I'd become so good at pretending that it really didn't matter to me anymore whether I had real girls' skates or not. And, come to think of it, the boys never did tease me anymore either. I'm not sure if it was because of Teddy's warning or something else.

Then last Christmas, the most amazing thing happened. I had opened all my gifts and I was so happy with everything I got. I was just getting up to go and try on a new outfit that Mom had bought me when she came back into the living room from the kitchen. She had her hands behind her back with this strange, sneaky smile on her face.

"Looks like Santa has one more present for you, Joanne," she teased and then she giggled.

Then I saw Teddy smirking behind her.

What's going on? Mom was acting really strange.

Then she pulled a big box out from behind her back. It looked like it had been quickly wrapped. I was still confused, but I was excited, too. She held the box out toward me. *What could it possibly be?* She was making such a big deal about it. I knew it had to be something really good. *But what? I had already gotten a whole bunch of great gifts.*

I took the gift from her and almost dropped it. It was a lot heavier than I'd expected. I ripped off the wrapping paper and tore open the box. And there they were. My very first pair of girls' skates!

"I know they're a little dirty and scuffed right now, but we'll clean them up and use some white polish on them and they'll look as good as new," Mom said.

"Can we do it now?" I blurted out.

"Let's get all this mess cleaned up first."

My mom had been right. Well, sort of. When we cleaned the skates and put the white polish on them, they looked a lot better. I didn't mind that they weren't new. All that mattered was that they were girls' and they were mine! When I tried them on, they were a little big for me, but once I put on two pairs of my brother's thick socks, they fit perfectly.

Thinking back now, I was glad they'd been extra big when I first got them. I tried them on last week and they fit me just right now, so I would be able to wear them again this winter.

And I was right, too. I remember that first day when I arrived at the school rink with my new skates. A lot of my girlfriends were there and they all said how happy they were that I finally had girls' skates. None of them said anything about the fact that they weren't new. I didn't care, and I was glad they didn't either. I couldn't wait to get on the ice and try them out. And when I did, I was sure I was skating so much better—so much more gracefully. It was just like when I pretended to have them. Having girls' skates really did make all the difference in the world.

As I lay there in bed thinking about my skates, I became excited about winter coming. *But it's going to be at least another month before it's cold enough to skate. I just have to put it out of my mind for now.*

Then I heard my sisters getting out of bed, so I figured I might as well get up, too.

Mom left after breakfast and I went out to play with my friends. I had only come home once during the day to grab a sandwich and go to the bathroom, so I barely paid attention to the fact that my mom wasn't there.

When I came home later in the day, my brother Kevin was sitting at the kitchen table with one of my mom's bar friends.

In the past couple of years, it had become a regular thing that my mom would go out to the bar drinking on Fridays after work. Sometimes, she would call us several times from the bar, each time saying she would be home in an hour. But I didn't mind. When she stayed out later, we got to have hotdogs for supper or something else that was easy to make and delicious to eat. And she usually came home in a happy mood. But not always.

Sometimes she would be crying and saying bad things about herself. She would say how no man would ever love her again now that she had only one breast or now that she was so fat. When she talked like that, it scared me.

Then there were other Fridays when she would bring home a friend to stay the night. She was always happy when that happened. At least at the time, that is. Sometimes I would hear her crying in bed the next morning after the friend left. That would scare me, too.

But lots of the time, she would be happy, and that made me happy. She would joke around with us more and she was more fun. So most of the time, I liked Friday nights.

But this was Saturday and Mom was away.

"Hey, Kevin. Hi, Greg," I said as I came into the kitchen.

"Hey, Jo," Kevin said.

"Hi, Joanne," Greg said. They both seemed really happy.

"Where's Mom?" I asked, thinking that she must have changed her mind about going away overnight.

"She's away until tomorrow. You knew that," Kevin answered.

"I just thought—." I looked over at Greg.

"Greg just dropped by to see Mom. He didn't realize she wasn't here."

"You don't mind if I stay awhile and visit you kids, do you?" he asked.

"No," I answered slowly, feeling confused. *Why would I mind?*

"Course not," Kevin reassured him.

I sat down at the table as Kevin drank something from Mom's shot glass.

"What's that?" I asked.

"It's vodka," Greg answered and then he emptied the whole shot glass in one gulp.

"You want another shot?" he asked Kevin.

"Sure," Kevin answered.

Greg poured a shot from the big bottle of vodka and slid it across the table to Kevin. He gulped it back and then made a face and jerked his head. We all started laughing at his reaction.

We sat there for a while, talking and laughing and having a really good time. It was a lot of fun spending time with Kevin. He was usually out with his friends, so I was really happy we could hang out together like that.

Then I suddenly had a thought. "Can I try it?" I asked as casually as I could. I didn't want them to know how nervous I was.

"You're too young," Kevin said.

"No she's not, Kevin," Greg said.

"No I'm not," I chimed in, trying to sound calm.

"You won't like it," Kevin said.

"Are you sure you want to try it?" Greg asked.

"I'm tellin' you. You won't like it," Kevin said.

"Why don't we just let her have a little sip?" Greg said.

I suddenly felt nervous. I had never drunk pure alcohol before. Oh, I'd tried a sip of my mom's beer, but I knew this was a lot stronger. She had told us about different types of alcohol and that vodka was hard liquor. That meant that it was a lot stronger than beer or wine and made a person drunk a lot faster.

I had never been drunk and I wasn't sure I would like it. But I knew that adults liked getting drunk and my brothers liked drinking, so I wanted to be grown up, too. I wanted to show Kevin that I wasn't a little kid anymore. *But what if he's right? What if I don't like it?*

What if I spit it out and look like a little baby? What if they laugh at me?

I was determined to prove to them that I wasn't a little kid and that I could drink just like a grown-up, so when I picked up the shot glass, I took a deep breath and gulped the whole thing back. I felt it burn my mouth and throat as I swallowed, but I didn't dare show any reaction. I just kept holding my breath until the burning had stopped.

"Holy shit, Jo!" Kevin said. I could hear the pride in his voice.

And then I felt the burning turn to a warmth inside and I liked how it made me feel.

We were all laughing and I felt so pleased with myself. Kevin said he was proud of me and they both said how amazed they were that I didn't even flinch. I was so glad I hadn't scrunched up my face the way I felt like doing. The way Kevin had done.

A little while later, I asked if I could have another shot.

"You better not, Jo. You'll get drunk and I'll get in trouble for letting you," Kevin said.

"No I won't, and I won't tell. Honest," I pleaded.

"She'll be okay, Kevin."

"I don't know," he replied slowly. But I could tell he wasn't arguing all that hard.

"Maybe just a half one?" I suggested.

"Well, okay. Just a half."

The half shots were much easier to swallow, and they didn't burn near as bad as the full shot had. I wasn't sure how many I'd drunk before I started to feel dizzy. And when I got up to go to the bathroom, my legs felt like rubber. I started to collapse onto the floor, but Kevin grabbed me and held me up. I flopped back onto the chair and leaned my head forward to rest it on my arms. I suddenly felt so heavy and really dizzy.

"You better go and sleep it off, Jo," Kevin said slowly.

"Why don't I help her upstairs," Greg offered.

Everything sounded slow to me. And distant. Their voices sounded muffled. I felt someone lift me up and carry me upstairs. Then I was lying on a bed and someone was starting to take off my clothes.

"I'm okay. I can change myself," I said, my words slurring.

I wasn't going to let anyone see me without clothes on, no matter how fuzzy I was feeling. Then I was in my room with my nightgown on. I flopped onto my bed and the room starting spinning. As the room spun me around and around, I started to feel sick. I pulled myself up from the bed and the spinning wasn't as bad. Suddenly I realized that I was going to be sick. I moved as quickly as I could to the bathroom and made it just in time.

When I came out of the bathroom, still feeling dizzy but a little better, Greg was standing there.

"Are you okay?" he asked.

"Yeah. I just want to go to bed."

"Why don't you sleep in your mom's bed. You'll be more comfortable in there," he said, holding my hand and leading me down the hall.

As I snuggled into my mom's bed, I heard him say something about checking on me later and then everything went black.

It felt like only a few minutes had gone by when I slowly started to wake up. But as I squinted my eyes open, I saw that it was pitch dark and realized I must have been sleeping a long time. I still felt dizzy and everything was foggy. I kept opening and shutting my eyes as I woke up.

Suddenly, my eyes flew open and my body stiffened! And then I felt the pain. There was someone on the bed behind me, touching me. The person was touching my private parts and it hurt. I froze in terror. *What's going on? Who's doing this to me?* I tried to pull away, but the person held me tight. I couldn't move.

And then I smelled him. I recognized his smell. It was Greg! My mom's friend Greg. *Why is he doing this? What did I do to make him do this to me? Please stop. Please don't do this to me. What are you doing? Why are you doing this? I'm just a kid. Don't you understand? I'm just a kid.*

I didn't know what to do. How could I make him stop? I had to get away. But how? He wouldn't let me go. I felt like I was going to be sick. I wanted to shout out but I couldn't. I was too terrified. *What if he gets mad at me? What will he do then?*

As he shifted his position, I could feel something hard pressing up against my bum. I panicked and, with more force than I knew I had, I pulled away.

"No!" I pleaded, as I fell to the floor with a thump.

"Shh," he whispered.

I scrambled to get up and heard him warn me not to tell anyone. He said I would be sorry if anyone found out, in a voice I had never heard from him before. I didn't want to know what he meant. That voice said it all. I ran out of my mom's room and into the bathroom to be sick.

After I was sick, I lay there on the bathroom floor, terrified to leave the safety of the locked room. But I was so tired, too. I crawled over to the door and sat there trying to figure out what I should do next. A short while later, I heard the sound of Greg snoring, but I was still too frightened to leave the bathroom. So I curled up into a ball by the door and listened. And when I was finally certain he was asleep, I cried.

I spent most of the night in the bathroom, but eventually I felt brave enough to come out and go into my own bed.

I woke up to the sound of my mom shouting, "What's she doing in bed at this time of day?" I still wasn't quite awake yet, but I caught pieces of Kevin and Teddy and my mom talking just outside my bedroom door.

"Why the hell would you let Greg stay here when I was away?" I heard her asking.

Terror gripped me instantly and then my mom was standing in the doorway.

"What were you thinking, Joanne?"

"I don't know," I groaned. I wasn't sure what she was talking about.

"Did he do something to you? Did he touch you?"

Oh no! How could she possibly know? Maybe she's just guessing. But how? Why would she even suspect? What if she found out the truth?

And then I thought about what he had said. "No, Mom. He didn't do anything."

I wanted so badly to run into her arms and tell her what had happened. I wanted her to tell me that everything was okay. I wanted her to reassure me that she still loved me now. I wanted her to tell me that I was a good girl. That I didn't do anything wrong. But I couldn't. I knew it wasn't true. If she knew what had happened, she would be mad at me. She would hate me. He was her friend. I'd ruined everything. I should never have gotten drunk. It was my fault this happened.

"Well maybe this will teach you not to drink," she said.

She started to walk away and then stopped and came back to the door of my room.

"Are you sure he didn't do anything?" she asked again.

"I'm sure, Mom," I said quietly.

She paused for a moment and then said, "You should really get up and try to have something to eat. It will make you feel better."

And so I did.

In the days and weeks after, I still couldn't tell anyone what had happened. I was too afraid. Afraid of what might happen. Afraid of what people would think of me. So I kept mostly to myself, avoiding even my closest friends. I tried hard not to think about it, but it kept playing over and over in my head like a bad dream. And each day, when I got home from school, I hesitated before going in the house. I looked around to make sure his car was nowhere nearby.

I couldn't even talk to William about it. I was too ashamed. In fact, I didn't speak to William at all until several weeks later. Not until after my Grampa died.

It was a few days before, when I first realized that something terrible was wrong. Grampa had fallen and broken his hip and was in the hospital. As I lay in bed trying to fall asleep, I overheard my mom talking on the phone to my uncle. She was crying and saying that she didn't think he was going to make it.

Then I felt this horrible dread wash over me. I was in a panic. *What if she's right? He can't die. He's my Grampa.* I loved him and I couldn't bear the thought of losing him. Of him being dead.

And then I thought, *what does "dead" really mean? What will happen to him if he's dead? Where will he go?* I knew we would never see him again, but where would he go?

Then I heard my mom saying, "Maybe you're right. I guess I am overreacting. I'm just so afraid of losing him. But you're right. I'm sure he'll be fine."

Thank goodness. I felt so relieved, but there was still this frightening dread inside me.

Three days later, my Grampa died.

When I heard, terror gripped me instantly. It was real. He was really gone. They couldn't take it back. They couldn't fix him—make him not dead anymore. I would never see him again. It was forever. The thought of forever was frightening. I was so terrified, I couldn't even cry. I could barely breathe.

In the next few days leading up to the funeral, there were all kinds of people that kept dropping in to our house. They all talked about Grampa and I didn't want to hear about it. I tried to stay in my room as much as possible. I didn't like them talking about my Grampa being dead. And Mom would cry. Every time someone new would come to visit, my mom would cry again. I didn't like it. It scared me. I didn't want to think about Grampa being dead.

And I still hadn't cried. If I cried, then it would be real. I didn't want it to be real, so I didn't cry.

On the day of the funeral, they put us in a room with my Grampa's coffin. I hated it. It was a small room to the side of a bigger room. There was nowhere in the room where you couldn't see him lying in the coffin. I didn't want to see him dead. It scared me. I couldn't turn my back to him, because that would leave me staring at a wall. So I tried to hide behind other people. But they kept moving in and out of the coffin room and every time they moved, I would catch a glimpse of my Grampa again.

Every time I saw him lying there, I got more and more frightened. Then Teddy came over to me and said I was supposed to go up and touch Grampa. *Is he nuts?*

Teddy explained that if you touch a dead person, it will prevent you from dreaming about them later. I had always trusted my big brother. He would never lie to me. And then I thought about being doomed to dream about my Grampa's dead body for the rest of my life. Suddenly that was more terrifying than the thought of touching him.

"Come on, Jo. We'll do it together. Whaddaya say?"

He took my hand and led me over to the coffin. I stood on the stool in front and looked down at him. It kinda looked like him but different. Teddy reached out and touched him.

"Now you do it, Jo. You'll feel a lot better after you do. Go on, Jo. Touch him."

I reached out and touched my Grampa and quickly pulled my hand away. He felt hard, not like a real person. He didn't really look like a real person anymore, either.

Panic hit me instantly and, as I turned to run out of the coffin room, I saw a man pulling the curtain across to separate us from all the people in the bigger room. As the terror gripped me, I looked around for another escape, but all the family was starting to sit down. My mom called me over and told me to sit next to her.

All the chairs faced the coffin, but my uncle was sitting in front of me, so I couldn't see my Grampa. I was so grateful for that. Then everyone was quiet and the man closed the lid on my Grampa's coffin. The silence was frightening and, before I knew what was happening, I began to cry uncontrollably. And once I started, I couldn't stop. I sobbed and sobbed.

"I'm sorry, Mom. I can't stop." I was so afraid that I was ruining the funeral.

"It's okay, honey. This is the time to cry. Just let it out."

And then my mom was crying and in the background I could hear others crying, too.

When the room became quiet again and I was still crying, my mom started to cry again.

"Maybe I shouldn't have brought her," she said. "She's too young for this. I shouldn't have let her come. But she loved her grandfather so much. I thought it would be good for her."

"She'll be okay. She just needs to get it out. She'll be fine in a little while. You'll see," I heard my uncle reassuring my mom.

Eventually, I did stop crying, more from exhaustion than anything. I still felt frightened and sad, but I just had no more energy for tears.

When we got back to my uncle's house after the funeral, my mom lay me down in one of my cousin's rooms for a rest. I was glad to finally be by myself for a while. I felt so tired I could barely keep my eyes open.

When I woke up later, it took me a minute to realize where I was. I must not have slept very long, because I saw that the sun was still quite bright outside. I could hear a lot of talking and laughter in the house. I wasn't ready to face the rest of the people, so I just lay there relaxing in the quiet of the room.

Hello, dear one. And how are you on this glorious day?

William. I'm glad you're here. And then I thought for a moment. *I've missed you.*

We are always with you, dear child. You know that.

But I haven't talked to you in a long time. I missed talking to you.

That is true. You have been busy. And we ask again, how are you on this fine day?

Not good. My Grampa died.

Ah but, dear child, your grandfather is not dead. He has simply moved out of your physical experience.

What do you mean?

There is no death. Life is infinite. We thought you understood that.

But then, where is my Grampa now? And then I thought about the funeral, about my Grampa lying in the coffin, dead.

We can feel your confusion. Your grandfather is no longer in his physical body. So we understand that you consider him dead. But that is not true.

But I saw him. I saw his dead body. He is dead.

You believe he is dead because his spirit no longer resides in that body. But his spirit is alive and well.

It is? Then I thought about what William had just said. *So then where is my Grampa, if he isn't dead? Where did he go?*

He is with us. And we are with you. So he is also with you.

Now I was really confused. *So does that mean he is in heaven? Does that mean you are in heaven, too?*

That is a good enough comprehension for now.

If you are in heaven, then does that mean that you are dead, too?

Dear little one. You must understand that there is no death. For anyone.

I started to feel a little reassured. I didn't like to think of my Grampa as being dead. *But will I ever see my Grampa again?*

Of course you will, sweet child.

Then I thought of something else. *If my Grampa is with you, then how is he feeling?*

He is feeling full of love and joy. Can you feel him? Try to feel him, dear one.

As I lay there trying to feel my Grampa, I started to feel the familiar warmth of William's love wash over me. I couldn't specifically feel my Grampa, though. *But I don't feel my Grampa. I thought you said he is with you.*

He is, dear one. He is. Just feel the love. Feel the joy. Feel our love for you. Feel your grandfather's love for you. Can you feel it?

Suddenly, that wonderful feeling of love and joy was so strong it no longer mattered whether I could recognize my Grampa specifically. I trusted William and if they said that my Grampa was with them, I believed them. If they said that my Grampa was alive and happy, then I believed them. *Thank you, William. I love you so much.*

Our love for you is greater than you know.

Chapter 16

The next four years felt like an emotional roller coaster for me. Not all of the time, but quite a lot of it. I purposely didn't talk to William about what had happened with Greg back then. I still felt too ashamed.

Looking back now, I realize that I was never quite the same after that day. I never did tell anyone what happened, but I still couldn't get it out of my mind. I found myself thinking about boys differently. And for the longest time, I looked at my mom's friends differently, too—I didn't trust them. And now I understood what my mom meant that day, that day when I was nine and I first came on my period.

It was shortly after that day that I found myself drifting away from a lot of my friends. Most of them seemed so young to me all of a sudden. We were all the same age, but I felt like I was much older than them.

For instance, I was deeply in love with James, my brother Kevin's best friend, and had been for quite some time, but most of my friends weren't even interested in boys yet. So I felt like I had no one to talk to about him. Or about so many other things I'd become interested in.

Then one day when I was hanging out with my friend Diana, I realized that she and I were able to talk about boys and life and all kinds of topics that appealed to me. She'd been spending a lot more of her time hanging out with girls that were older than us, and I envied her for that. I yearned to be able to spend more time with people that understood me. That had the same interests as I had.

"You're lucky," I said, after listening to her tell me about the day before, when she'd been hanging out with a couple of older girls.

"What do you mean?" she asked.

"It must be nice to hang out with girls that aren't still just kids."

"Well, you can too, if you want," she replied.

"Yeah but they don't really know me. I'm sure they won't want to hang out with me. They'll probably think I'm still a little kid, too."

"No they won't. I'll tell them you're not. The next time we're hanging out, you can come with me."

"Really? That would be great. Thanks, Diana."

"No problem. I like hanging out with you and I know they will, too."

I'd always liked Diana. She was such an outgoing person and I tended to be rather shy and quiet. And she seemed to like me, too. I was a good listener and she was a good talker, so we made a good pair.

I had a sudden thought. I took a deep breath and blurted out, "Do you think we could be best friends?" I didn't give her a chance to answer. I didn't want her to automatically say no. Seeing as how we're so much more mature than the other kids our age, it would be nice to hang out together all the time, don't you think?" I held my breath and waited for what seemed like an eternity, but it was really only a second or two.

"Sure. That sounds like a great idea," she answered.

I couldn't believe my ears! She said yes. I had a best friend. And not just any best friend. She was very popular, and hanging around with Diana would make me popular, too. The truth is, I knew I was kind of popular myself, but that was because of my big brothers. They were both really popular, so people tended to be nice to me because of them. It crossed my mind that Diana might have said yes because she had a crush on Teddy, but I didn't care. All that mattered was that we were best friends now.

Diana and I became inseparable. We were in the same class and we hung out all the time, both in school and outside of school. We walked to and from school together every day, and she would hang out at my house when we weren't outside with other friends. During the summer, I went away for a two-week vacation with her and her parents to a cabin they rented every year. Her dad jokingly called us Mutt and Jeff. Diana was five foot nothing, and I was already five foot six inches tall.

I hated being so tall. But I didn't mind her dad joking about it. I knew he liked me and I knew he wasn't making fun of me or being mean. He had a great sense of humour and we joked around a lot together. I would simply tease him back by patting the top of his head. He was barely any taller than Diana.

We had even become popular with the teachers at school, always helping out with special projects and activities. So when our music teacher encouraged us to try out for the school musical, *Tom Sawyer*, we were both quick to say we would.

I was nervous, though. I didn't think I was a very good singer, even though I had always dreamed of miraculously waking up one day with a beautiful singing voice. It never happened, though.

As I sat there waiting for my turn to audition, I became more and more nervous. Some of the girls had such strong, beautiful voices. By the time I got up to sing my song, I was so nervous I was ready to back out. But my music teacher and her friend, who was helping out by directing the play, started to root me on and then I didn't want to let them down by quitting. So I sang my heart out. My voice wasn't as loud and strong as the other girls, but it wasn't awful either.

A few days later, we found out that we had both been chosen for the play. I couldn't believe it! And then I found out I'd been chosen to play one of the witches. *Oh great. That's just rich. Well then, if I'm going to be a witch, I'm going to be the best darn witch of them all.*

*

We'd been rehearsing for over a week, and every time the three of us witches did our song, the director kept shouting, "Louder, louder!"

Then she explained that we were supposed to be threatening. That we weren't supposed to have these sweet voices.

When I sang my solo piece again, still trying to sing with as beautiful a voice as I could, she shouted out, "Remember, you are mean. You are scary. Make me believe you are a frightening witch. Louder. Louder. Now let's take it from the top."

I was so embarrassed standing up there on the stage, with her bellowing at me. And then I got angry. *If she wants a loud, scary witch, I'll give her loud and scary. I don't care if she kicks me out of the play. I'll show her how stupid it will sound.*

So we started over again and when it was my turn to sing the solo part, I stepped forward. I made an ugly, menacing face and bellowed out my piece of the song in a loud, screeching voice that echoed through the gym. When I was finished, I took a deep breath and braced myself for her anger.

But instead, she came storming up to the stage exclaiming, "You've got it. That was perfect! That's exactly what I want."

I couldn't believe it. She actually liked it. No—she loved it. And everyone else did, too. They were all laughing and patting me on the back and saying how great I was.

As the weeks went by, I perfected my song and added actions to my part that emphasized that I was this wicked, wicked witch.

My friends kept telling me I was the highlight of the show. So, by the time opening night came and all our parents and families had come to see us, I was feeling really excited.

Then it was my turn to go on and I felt like I did my best performance ever. When I went back stage afterward, everyone complimented me on how good I was. It was thrilling. I couldn't wait to find out what my mom thought.

Later that evening, we all piled into my mom's car to go home. My mom said how good the musical was, but she hadn't said anything about my part.

"So how did you like my part?" I asked.

"It was awfully loud. And I couldn't understand a word you were saying."

I was crushed. "It was supposed to be that way," I explained.

"I'm sorry, but you asked what I thought. Don't be so defensive."

"Everyone else thought I was great."

"I'm not saying you weren't good. I guess I just don't appreciate that kind of performance."

"Obviously not," I huffed. And then I fell silent for the rest of the drive home. The excitement was gone. *Why couldn't she just say it was good? Why did she have to be so critical? If Carl had seen it, he would have liked it. I'm sure of it. Carl likes everything I do.*

Carl was my mom's boyfriend. He'd been living with us for quite a while now. I really loved him. And he loved me. He was nothing like that creep she'd lived with before. George was mean.

Even Teddy and Kevin hated him. And for me, it was not because I didn't trust any adult male.

I thought about what Greg had done to me all those years before and shuddered. Ever since Greg had molested me when I was ten, I couldn't be in the same room with an adult man by myself. I was afraid of them. Afraid of what they might do to me. Even when they were nice to me, I didn't trust them. I was afraid they would do the same thing Greg had done.

Initially, it was the same with Carl. I remember the first time I found myself in a room with him, and I started to leave.

"Where are you going Jo?" he had asked.

"Just into the kitchen," I answered, a little too quickly. I felt my face turning red.

He looked at me and seemed confused. "Can you grab me a beer?"

What am I going to do now? I can't say no. He'll know something's wrong.

"Okay," I said reluctantly.

I brought him the beer and started to dart back into the kitchen.

"Say, Jo. Why don't you come and sit here next to me so we can chat for a bit?" He patted the spot next to him on the couch.

No. I don't want to. You might try to hurt me.

"It's okay, Jo. I won't bite."

I started to panic. *Oh no. He can read my mind.* I didn't know what else to do, so I went over and sat on the chair across from him, rather than beside him. And we talked. Just talked.

It took several more times spending time alone with Carl before I came to trust him. Carl was different. He was good to me and I finally realized that not all men wanted to physically abuse me. Carl loved me as a person. I felt safe with Carl. I felt better just thinking about him.

But Carl was away for work, so he couldn't make it to my musical that night. *I wish he could've been here. I know she wouldn't have been so critical if he was here. He wouldn't have let her. He always jumps to my defence whenever she's being hard on me.*

And then I remembered the time I overheard them talking. "Why are you always defending her?" she was saying.

"Because somebody has to."

"What do you mean?"

"It's obvious that Shirley is your favourite daughter. And you make it so obvious to her, too."

"I do not. I've never said that to her."

"You don't have to say it. She knows."

"Well, I can't help it. Shirley is my little baby. Why shouldn't I love her?"

"I'm not saying you shouldn't love Shirley. But can't you see what an incredible little girl Joanne is? And smart, too? You just don't seem to realize how special she is."

"Of course I realize it. All my children are special. And I love them all."

But Carl was right—I did know. I knew my mom loved Shirley the most. I also understood how my mom felt, though. And I didn't resent my baby sister Shirley. How could I? She was a sweet, quiet, beautiful little girl who you couldn't help but love.

At least Carl loves me. We pulled into our driveway.

Once I got back to school the next day and everyone was still talking about how great the musical had been and what a great job I had done, I was easily able to put my mom's comments out of my mind. Even my teachers said I gave a great performance, so I felt good all over again.

*

During the week, we usually hung out at the store closest to the school, so all of us could be together. Some of us lived quite far from school, but a lot of our friends lived in the neighbourhood right by the school, so this worked out best for everyone. And today was no different.

As we hung out at the store after school, I was still feeling the glow of my success in the musical when Tommy came by and asked if he could hang out with us.

Tommy was our classmate, Brad's younger brother. He was a good kid and we didn't mind him hanging out with us.

I gave him a playful slap on the shoulder and said, "No problem."

He beamed in appreciation. "Thanks Joanne."

A little while later, a bunch of the guys showed up and we all said our usual hellos.

Then John showed up and asked, "What are you doin' here, Tommy? Why don't you go on and find some of your little friends to play with?"

I looked over at Tommy. He looked crushed. I thought he was going to cry. "Knock it off, John. We said he could stay. Don't listen to him, Tommy."

"But he's just a kid," John argued.

"Look, he's not bothering anyone. If you don't like it, then take off."

John could see that nobody else was jumping in to agree with him, so he backed off.

I looked over at Tommy and gave him a smile and a wink.

He suddenly had the biggest, proudest grin on his face and I felt so pleased that I had made him feel like one of the gang. I remembered how it felt to want so badly to hang out with older kids. And now that I was the older kid, I felt the need to protect Tommy from idiots like John.

I did like John. But he could be a bit of a jerk sometimes. He didn't have any brothers or sisters, so he didn't understand that it was okay to hang around kids of different ages.

It was a couple of hours later before we all dispersed to go home for supper. It was Friday, so we all agreed to meet back at the store a little later to hang out for the evening.

When I got close to home, I saw Carl's truck out in front of the house, and I started to run. He'd been away for the last three days and I'd missed him. As I ran up the driveway, I could hear them out in the backyard. Rather than go in the house first, I headed straight for the yard.

"There's my girl," he said as I walked into the backyard.

"Why don't you put your school books in the house," Mom said as I gave Carl a hug and kiss.

"But I want to visit with Carl for a bit."

"Leave her be, Bernie," he said.

Carl called my mom Bernie, even though that wasn't her real name. She didn't like the nickname and she wouldn't let anyone else call her that.

"So how did the musical go?" he asked.

"It was great. Everyone said my performance was fabulous."

"I knew it would be. I had every confidence that you would do a great job."

I glared over at my mom, as if to say, "I told you so." I could tell she was pissed off.

"Are you ready for another beer, Carl?" I said.

"Sure, honey. That would be great. You ready, Bernie?"

My mom held her beer up to see how much was left in the bottle. "Not yet," she said.

"Can I have one?" I asked hopefully.

This was my regular routine. I'd ask and Mom would say no. But it didn't stop me from asking again the next time.

"No," she answered.

I didn't expect anything else.

"Come on, Bernie. Let her have just one. To celebrate her performance."

"I don't want to encourage her. She's too young," she argued.

"One won't hurt her. And besides, I'd rather her drink with us than be out drinking with her friends where we can't keep an eye on them."

"Well, maybe just one," she agreed.

I couldn't believe it. She actually said yes! *She must be in a good mood because Carl's back and she missed him, too.*

I jumped up and ran into the house before she changed her mind. I decided to bring her one too, just in case she finished hers while I was gone. Besides, I wanted her to stay in a good mood, and another beer would definitely help.

And I was right. By the time I got back, she was almost finished and seemed pleased that I had brought her one, too.

We sat and talked as I drank my beer. I liked the taste of beer and I liked that it didn't get me drunk so quick. I was enjoying myself and had finished about half the bottle when Carl slapped his knee and told me to come and sit on his lap. And I happily did.

As I got comfortable on his lap and took another swig of my beer, he said, "I want to talk to you about something."

"What?" I asked pleasantly.

"Now I'm being serious."

But he didn't sound serious. "Okay, I'm listening," I said, trying to sound serious, but not succeeding.

"I mean it. This is serious."

But he still didn't sound it and so I laughed teasingly.

And then he laughed too. "Now come on, Jo. This is important."

But he was having a hard time keeping a straight face, and before long we were both chuckling.

"Okay. Can you go and get us another beer and then we'll talk."

"You mean me, too?" I asked.

"Sure, why not."

"No, Carl. She's already had one," my mom piped up.

I looked at Carl and gave him my pleading look.

"Go ahead, Jo," he said and gave me a wink.

As I jumped up and went into the house, I could hear them arguing about my having another beer. But it sounded more playful than anything. *Oh good. Mom is in a good mood.*

When I came back with the beers, I planted myself back on Carl's lap.

"Now listen, Jo. The thing I want to talk to you about is that your thirteenth birthday is coming up. And that means that you're going to be a teenager."

"Yeah?"

I didn't know what he was getting at. I looked over at my mother for a clue. She shrugged, rolling her eyes in Carl's direction as she stood, got her balance and staggered slightly toward the house.

"You know that you're a beautiful young lady now and I want to be sure that you continue to keep your innocence. Do you know what I'm talking about?"

"Yeah." Now I knew what he was getting at. *Do we really have to talk about this?*

"Jo, I'm really proud of you and I know that you wouldn't have sex with a boy till you're older, would you?"

"Of course not!"

"You're still a virgin, aren't you?"

"Carl, of course I am! Why would you wonder about that?"

"I knew you were. I just wanted to be sure."

"Well, I am."

"You know there are a lot of boys that only want one thing from a girl, and I just want to be sure that you respect yourself enough to not let them talk you into something you're not ready for."

"I won't."

"You know I love you and your mom loves you. And we want the best for you. You are such a beautiful girl and I want you to wait until you are older before you have sex with anyone."

"Don't worry. I am not going to let anyone ball me."

"Now that's the kind of thing I'm talking about."

"What do you mean?"

"I mean using the word "balling." It sounds cheap. You know, when you're older and in love with someone, it won't be just sex. You won't think of it as balling—you'll be making love."

I liked the sound of that. Making love. It sounded so grown up. So romantic. Then I thought of James, and I could feel my face turning red.

"Are you sure you haven't done anything yet? You wouldn't lie to me, would you?"

I was so embarrassed to have this conversation, but thankfully the beer helped to soften my embarrassment. And, I had to admit, I was also happy that Carl cared so much. I could tell that he was a little uncomfortable talking about this, too, but he cared enough about me to suffer through the awkwardness.

"No. Honest."

"I trust you. I respect you and I want you to respect yourself. If I ever found out that you had lost your virginity, I would be so disappointed in you."

"You don't need to worry. I won't. I promise."

"Good girl. I love you. You know that, don't you? I love you like a daughter. You know that?"

"I love you too," I said truthfully.

I felt so good. He considered me his daughter! I was so thrilled. Somehow, even though it was such an embarrassing discussion, it made me feel so loved that he would struggle through it just for me. And I had no intention of disappointing him. He loved me and I would never do anything to upset him or make him stop loving me. He was the father I never really had.

Later that night, after spending a fun evening with my friends, I settled into bed and pulled the blankets up under my chin to snuggle in and fall asleep.

Hello, luv. And how are you on this fine evening?

William! It's so good to hear from you. I wasn't even thinking about you.

We are pleased that you are pleased.

I had a great day!

We can tell. We feel your happiness.

You're right. I am happy. I had a great day at school and I had fun with my friends after. And then after that, I had a really nice time with Carl and my mom. And then I went out with my friends and we had fun again. It was a perfect day!

We are filled with your joy. And we are so appreciative of it.

I am so thankful, too. Everything's going so well for me right now.

Savour this feeling. Remember it and bask in it always.

But—

Do not hesitate. Do not doubt. You can always feel this way if you choose to.

What do you mean?

Your happiness is of your choosing.

I didn't agree with them, but I didn't want to argue. I was feeling too good and I didn't want to spoil my good feeling.

That's it. You've got it. We are so proud of you.

I didn't know what they were talking about. *What do you mean?*

You had a choice. And you chose happiness. We are pleased.

I couldn't help myself. I needed to understand. *But I'm happy because I had a good day. What about when I have a bad day? How can I choose to be happy on a bad day?*

You can choose to be happy no matter what experience you are having. The feeling of happiness is your choice. And your choice alone.

You're saying that I can be happy even when something bad has happened?

We are. Just as you did a moment ago.

When? I don't remember.

You chose happiness over disagreeing with us. And we could feel your emotional shift. We are very pleased with your awareness.

I thought about what they had said. Then I realized what they meant. I did choose to avoid arguing with them because I wanted to continue to feel good. I knew that if I started to talk about bad things, it would make me feel bad and I wanted to stay feeling happy. So I'd moved my thoughts back to pleasant ones.

We are very pleased with your growth. Can you feel our joy for you?

And I did. That familiar feeling of warmth and love filled me up from my toes all the way to the top of my head and deep, deep inside of me. I wanted to reach out and hold them. Hug them. But I didn't have to. It was as though they had wrapped themselves around me and inside of me with a feeling of joy that no words could describe.

Thank you so much, William. I love you. I love you so, so much.

Our love for you is greater than you know.

Chapter 17

I didn't realize at the time just how important that conversation with Carl really was to me, or how strong an impact it was going to have on the decisions I would make later on. He never brought up the subject again, but he didn't need to.

Over the next year, our bond grew stronger and stronger. And my mother and I continued to do battle more and more often. But not always—sometimes she could be fun and reasonable. And it was becoming harder to know which way a conversation or situation was going to go with her.

One Sunday afternoon, for instance, I was just stopping in to the house to grab a sandwich before going back out to meet Diana. As I walked into the house, Teddy whispered that I should stay clear of Mom.

"Why, what's up?" I asked.

"She's fuming, man."

"About what?"

Then he started to snicker.

What on earth did I do now to piss her off?

"Is that Joanne?" I heard her yelling from the basement.

Crap! Teddy was right. She sounds really pissed.

"Get down here, Joanne."

I looked back at Teddy, who was trying to stop himself from laughing. I was confused. Teddy was usually so supportive. *What the hell is going on?*

"I said get down here!"

"I'm coming," I shouted back and ran down the stairs, with Teddy following behind me.

I checked the rec room but she wasn't there. Teddy tugged at me and pointed to the back room. So I went into the laundry room. As I turned the corner, I saw my mom holding up a garbage bag. I took one look at her face and froze. She was furious.

"Do you know what this is?" she demanded.

"No."

And then I looked over at Teddy for some kind of clue. He was trying hard not to laugh, but I was so confused that I scrunched up my brows and asked, "What is it?"

"You know damn well what it is. I was so embarrassed when the repairman pulled it all out from behind the furnace."

I still didn't have a clue what she was talking about. Then she reached in the garbage bag and pulled out a handful of paper. As she held the paper out to me, a wad fell to the ground and a bunch of dried up peas spilled out onto the floor.

I instantly went into panic mode and as I felt my face turn beet red, I was sure she could tell. "It wasn't me."

"Don't try to deny it. I know it was you!" she yelled.

And then I made the mistake of looking back at Teddy.

He could barely contain himself. He looked like he was almost in pain, as he tried to hold back his laughter. I couldn't help myself. I broke into uncontrollable laughter. And that got Teddy laughing. The tears poured down my face and I could barely breathe. I crossed my legs to stop from peeing my pants. I glanced at my mom and she looked stunned.

"I'm sorry, Mom," I cried out through my laughter. I couldn't stop laughing, but I knew it was only going to make her more pissed off.

But then she looked over at Teddy and suddenly she was laughing, too.

She continued to try to scold me, but it had lost its effect. We were all laughing and the tears were flowing down our faces.

Later on, I admitted what I had done when I was younger and reassured her that I had stopped putting my vegetables down the hole a long time ago.

I was glad we could still have fun some of the time. It helped me get through the times when she was so unreasonable. And, of course, there was Carl. He always jumped to my defence and, because my mom loved him so much, he was often able to smooth things over.

It also helped that my mom liked Diana, and Diana really liked my mom. My mom didn't like a lot of my other friends at all, and she made no bones about pointing it out, every chance she got.

During our final year in public school, Diana and I had become more popular than ever. We had now become part of the cool group. In fact, we *were* the cool group. Everyone wanted to hang out with us. Outside of school hours, we often hung around older kids, which made us even more popular with the kids at school.

Tommy continued to hang out with us every chance he could. Over that year, we saw him blossom. I could tell that he looked up to Diana and me, and we really didn't mind him hanging around us at all. It made me feel good to know we had helped him come out of his shell. He was much happier and so much more confident.

John and some of the other boys had stopped bugging him, and his brother Brad had come to trust that he wouldn't tell on him to his parents, so even he no longer minded that Tommy was hanging out with our group. He had become part of the gang without anyone openly admitting it.

It was because of this that we were so frightened by what happened on that warm spring evening. It was a typical school night. A small group of us were hanging out at the store, and I was quietly telling Diana about the dream I had of her and this guy, Sam. Sam was a friend of Brad's from another school, who Diana had recently become interested in. I was right in the middle of telling her the dream when John and Paul came riding up on their bikes, yelling, "Brad. You gotta come."

"What's up?"

"Tommy's just been hit by a car!"

Terror gripped me instantly. Then everything seemed to move in slow motion. I looked over at Brad and he seemed stunned, confused. It was as if the information wasn't registering.

"Come on, Brad. We gotta go," John yelled out, breaking the eerie silence.

Brad started to move and the slow motion was replaced with panic and yelling. Everyone shouted out questions, and John shouted out answers, but they were all jumbled together. Brad jumped on the back of John's bike and they rode off, with the rest of us running to keep up. As we ran, I pleaded in my mind, *please let Tommy be okay. Please don't let him be hurt. Please. I beg you.*

When we came around the corner to Tommy's street, we could see a large crowd hovering around near the road in front of his neighbour's house. There were so many people crowded around him I couldn't get close enough to see him.

The truth is, I didn't want to see him. I was afraid. No—I was terrified. I couldn't bear to see our little Tommy lying there, hurt. Brad had pushed his way through the crowd and then came back out and walked over to the fence in front of a house a few doors down. A few of us followed him over and stood with him.

I looked into his face and instantly felt the pain and fear wash over me.

His head was swaying back and forth as he repeated, "Oh man. Oh man. Oh man." He was trying so hard to hold it together. To not cry. This was his little brother. Nothing could happen to him. This was little Tommy. He had to be okay.

I finally managed to blurt out, "He'll be okay, Brad. He has to be. He'll be okay."

And as I tried to reassure him, I realized I was also trying to reassure myself.

John came back out from the crowd and said, "He's going to be okay, Brad. It looks a lot worse than it really is. It's just all that blood that's making it look so bad."

What's he saying, "all that blood"? Is that supposed to make Brad feel better? Is that supposed to make us all feel better?

"He's okay, Brad. There's a nurse from down the street looking after him and he's talking and telling her what happened. He's really okay. Honest, man."

Then I suddenly realized it had been a long time since we'd got there and the ambulance still hadn't arrived. *Where the hell is the goddamn ambulance? They need to get him to the hospital.*

I was starting to panic. As if someone had read my mind, I heard the sound of the siren as the ambulance pulled onto the street. *Thank God they're here. Tommy's going to be fine after all.*

Relief washed over me. I could feel my whole body trembling, but I felt so relieved as I watched the ambulance pull away.

Once the ambulance was gone, the conversation switched to what had happened. Tommy'd been playing hide and seek with some friends when he stopped and sat on the curb to tie up his shoelace. A car came racing down the street and jumped the curb where Tommy was sitting. It dragged him quite a distance before swerving back onto the road, leaving Tommy lying there on the grass as it sped away.

The bloody creeps just left him there! They didn't even stop to see if he was okay.

Some of the older kids, including Teddy and Kevin, went searching the neighbourhood, hoping to spot the car. We also heard stories that there were three older teenagers in the car and that the car was stolen. A couple of neighbours said they'd heard the teenagers laughing as they sped away. By the end of the evening, the police still hadn't located the car or the teenagers.

I felt emotionally drained as I walked up the driveway to my house, so when I crawled into bed a short while later, I fell instantly into a deep sleep.

*

Diana and I were both anxious to get to school the next morning so we could get an update from Brad on how Tommy was doing. I had slept in, which meant we had to hurry if we wanted to get there before the bell rang. We didn't want to have to wait until recess to talk to him.

But when we rounded the corner into the schoolyard, we saw that everyone was already starting to line up to go into the school.

Damn! Now we were going to have to wait. We fell into line behind Pauline and I blurted out, "Did you hear about Tommy?" I hadn't seen her last night, so I figured she might not know yet what happened.

"He's dead," she said sadly.

"No you're wrong! We were there. He was fine when they took him to the hospital. He was talking and everything." *It's amazing how quickly the rumour mill gets started.*

"They had to rush him into surgery this morning and he died during the operation," she continued.

I felt sick to my stomach. *This can't be true. She got it wrong. He can't be dead.*

Suddenly Diana let out the most horrifying moan and went running into the girls' washroom, and I went running in after her. I still didn't believe it. *It can't be true.*

Diana threw herself on the washroom floor sobbing. I ran into one of the stalls and locked the door. *It's not true. It can't be true. It has to be a mistake. I refuse to believe it.*

A few minutes later, one of the female teachers came into the washroom and said, "I know you girls are upset about Tommy. Your teacher wanted me to check on you to make sure you're okay. It's alright. You can stay in here for a while. I'll come back in a little while to see how you're doing. We are all very sad about Tommy."

And then it hit me. *It's true. But it can't be.*

"Oh God, no!" I said, sobbing. As I continued to cry uncontrollably, I felt my whole body start to tremble. I jumped off the toilet seat and stuck my head over the bowl, just in time. I had stopped crying just long enough to vomit. And then I thought about our little Tommy and the sobbing started again. I just couldn't accept the finality of it. All his hopes and dreams, gone. He was just a little kid. *How could this happen to him?* And I cried some more.

And that's how most of the day went. The teacher came in to check on us every once in a while, and some of our other friends came in and out of the washroom to talk and cry and talk some more.

It was a short while after lunch when the teacher came back in to tell us that everyone was being sent home early. We were all too upset, including the teachers, to carry on with our school day.

"Go home and be with your families," she said, choking out the words as tears rolled down her face.

Tommy's funeral was held that weekend. Hundreds of people turned out for it, maybe more. It was a large church and people spilled out onto the street.

As I watched them carry his casket down the aisle and out of the church, I still couldn't fully accept that he was gone forever. That we would never see his smiling face again. That we would never see those big brown eyes staring up at us in admiration. We would never hear his contagious giggle again.

    *

It had been just over a week, and Brad still hadn't come back to school. Diana and I were sitting in the diner by the school with some of our friends when I saw Tommy's older sister Pam come in with two other girls.

I didn't know Pam very well. She was a few years older than we were so we didn't see that much of her. She hung out with my brothers sometimes, so we did see her on occasion, but not that often.

I didn't know what to say, so I avoided looking directly at her. I couldn't imagine how she was feeling. I couldn't even let myself try to think about how it would feel to lose one of my brothers or sisters. I couldn't bear it. It would kill me. Then every once in a while, I would sneak a peek in her direction. I expected to see the pain written all over her face. I expected to see her crying or trying hard not to. But instead, she looked normal. I couldn't tell what she was talking about, but she seemed to be acting normal. As if nothing had happened. *How can she look so normal when she's lost her little brother? Her little brother is dead. How can she just act as though it's a day like any other? Maybe she's just really good at hiding it?*

I don't think I could ever come out of the house again. I could never have a regular conversation again. I could never laugh again. Or hope and dream again. I don't think I could ever feel happy again if it was me.

*

As the days turned into weeks, I got more and more angry that they still hadn't found the creeps that had killed Tommy. *How can they possibly live with themselves? How can they go through life knowing that they killed a ten-year-old boy? I hope the guilt consumes them. Even if they never get caught, I hope they go through the rest of their lives thinking about what they've done. Hating themselves for what they've done.*

Often, I found myself pleading with William to make it be just a bad nightmare. To make me wake up and discover that it hadn't been real after all. But William never responded. And I never did wake up from the nightmare.

But then finally, eventually, I was able to get through a day without thinking about Tommy. It helped that we were busy planning and organizing our big end-of-year school trip. We'd decided that we all wanted to go to our teacher's campground for a weekend rather than go on the usual trip to the capital.

I had never been camping before, so I was really excited about it. All the cool teachers had volunteered to be chaperones. I couldn't wait. It was so amazing to think we were going to spend a whole weekend with all our friends and all the fun teachers. It was going to be like one big pyjama party but with girls and boys.

Finally, the day arrived and we all piled into the two school buses to head up to the campground. After we set up the tents and stored our things away, we helped the teachers barbeque hot dogs and hamburgers for supper.

When it got dark, we made a huge bonfire. Our music teacher had brought her guitar, so we all sat around the fire singing songs and roasting marshmallows. It was even better than I had imagined it would be.

Over the course of the evening, a group of us had quietly arranged to meet later to have a seance once the adults had turned in for the night. After all, we couldn't spend the weekend camping without a seance, could we?

Later that night, we all gathered at the tent that was being used to store our luggage and extra sleeping bags. It was a huge tent, so we could all fit in it easily. There were fourteen of us and, before I knew it, they'd talked me into leading the seance. Most of my closest friends knew about my dreams and they figured I'd be the best one.

Some of my girlfriends and I had done it before when I had sleepovers, so I knew what I was supposed to do. We all sat in a circle on the ground, held hands and closed our eyes. Shortly after we started, I opened my eyes and it was as though I was the only one there. My friends seemed to have faded away. I looked over at the luggage and sleeping bags piled high in the tent. And there was Tommy, sitting up on top of the pile! I couldn't believe my eyes.

"Tommy, is that you?"

"It is," he replied.

But he sounded strange. Older. "Are you okay, Tommy?"

"I am wonderful."

Something felt strangely familiar to me about Tommy. But it didn't feel like Tommy.

"And how are you?" he asked.

Then I recognized the voice. He had the same feel to him that I'd get when I talked to William.

"Is that you, William?"

"It's me, Tom."

It looked like Tommy, but it felt more like William. Is William playing a trick on me? No. They would never do that. But

Tommy felt so much older than his ten years. And wiser. He felt wise, like William felt to me.

"We all miss you, Tommy."

"Please tell Brad not to worry about me. Tell him I'm fine. I'm happy and I want him to be happy, too."

As I thought about Tommy being dead, I couldn't help wondering how he could possibly be happy. How can a dead person be happy? And then I had a thought. This was my big chance to finally find out. I was afraid to know, but I couldn't help myself. I had to ask. "Tommy? What's it like to be dead?"

And he was gone.

I suddenly realized I had my eyes closed, and I became aware that people were shaking me and calling my name. I opened my eyes and stared up into the faces of my friends. They were all terrified. And then they looked relieved.

"What's going on?" I just assumed they had all been watching Tommy and me have our conversation. But instead, they said I'd been in a trance and they couldn't pull me out of it.

"What happened?" they all asked.

So I told them. And then I started to doubt myself. *Had I really been talking to Tommy? Or was it William? Had they shown me Tommy's face and body because they knew how much I wanted to see him? No, they wouldn't do that. But maybe they didn't realize that what they were doing was wrong. No that's stupid. William knows everything. Of course they would know. It had to be Tommy. But he seemed so different. And why wouldn't he answer my question? Was it because he knew I wouldn't like the answer?*

Then I got scared. *What if being dead is horrible and he didn't want to tell me? But he said he was happy. He told me to tell Brad that he was happy and not to worry about him. So why wouldn't he tell me, then?*

I didn't like the way I was feeling, so I tried to think about something else. I looked over at my friends and saw that some of the boys were starting to laugh and goof around. The distraction was just what I needed. I started to laugh, too, and as I did, I could feel myself relaxing. I felt much better.

The rest of the weekend flew by and we all had such a good time. Except for the seance. I still had mixed feelings about my meeting with Tommy, but I just tried to put it out of my mind the best I could. And for the most part, I did.

When I got home from my camping trip, I found out that my mom and Carl had broken up. They had often had fights before and broken up, but this time it seemed different. I could tell that my mom had been crying a lot. That wasn't the different part, though. Carl had packed up all his things and taken them with him. He'd never done that before. Mom said he'd gone back to his ex-wife and family.

Over the next few weeks, I kept expecting to see his truck out in front of the house when I came home. But it never was. I didn't understand it. *Why didn't he contact me? He didn't even call to say goodbye. I thought he loved me. If he loved me, he would've still kept in touch. Just because he and Mom broke up, didn't mean that he had to leave me, too. He could've at least called.*

Chapter 18

The school year was almost over, and Diana had been going around with Sam for three weeks now. I hated it when Diana had a boyfriend. I always felt like a third wheel. In fact, I was a third wheel. Or sometimes worse. Sometimes her boyfriend would bring one of his friends with him. That was definitely worse. It was so obvious that they were trying to set me up, and that made me really uncomfortable.

Often the guys were real dorks, and I was stuck hanging out with them while Diana and her boyfriend were wrapped in each other's arms, kissing and whispering and giggling together. But it was even worse when they were cute and nice. The good-looking ones never liked me. I felt so awkward around them. I never knew what to say, so I would crawl into my shell and say nothing. I hated being so ugly.

Two weeks later, our summer holidays were finally here, and Diana had just broken up with Sam the week before. I was glad. It may have been selfish to think that way, but I knew it would be a long, lousy summer if she had a steady boyfriend. The two of us had so much fun together when she wasn't going around with anyone. But when she had a boyfriend, it was all about him. And her. I knew it was a flaw in her character and I just accepted it, for the most part. I also knew that I would never do the same to her, but I didn't have to worry about that.

I had never had a boyfriend and I didn't expect that to change any time soon.

Besides, I was still deeply in love with James, and he had made it quite clear that he couldn't go out with me because of my brother. He was my brother's best friend, and I was Kevin's little sister. That was a real no-no.

I knew he was flattered that I was in love with him, but I could never be sure whether he was interested in me or just using my brother as an excuse to avoid hurting my feelings.

One time a few months earlier, he'd been drinking, and he started necking with me. It was so incredible. I felt like I was in heaven. I thought for sure that he really liked me. But then he pulled away and said he couldn't do it—Kevin would be furious.

So there we were, sitting at my kitchen table on our first night of the summer. My brothers were having a party downstairs to celebrate the end of the school year because my mom was down at Grandma's cottage for the weekend. And that meant a lot of their older friends would be coming up from the basement to go to the washroom.

Diana was spending the night, as usual. We just loved when my brothers had their parties. Every time someone would come up to go to the bathroom, we would ask for a swig of their beer. No one seemed to mind, either. And the drunker they got, the more generous they got. It never seemed to occur to them that we were having drinks from everyone's beer.

And of course, there were all the hunks! My brothers had a lot of gorgeous friends. But most of all, I hoped that James was down there. Every time I heard someone coming up the stairs, I prayed that it was James. I kept hoping he would get drunk and kiss me again.

A short while later, Kevin came up to the kitchen and plopped himself down in the chair beside Diana. That wasn't unusual. Kevin often sat and gabbed with me. Mostly it was when we were home on our own, but he would also sit and talk with me or us when he needed a break from his friends downstairs. I loved the fact that he talked to me as his equal. He hardly ever treated me like a little kid, even though he was older.

"Hey, Kevin," we both chimed in.

"Hey, Jo. Hey, Diana. Whatcha up to?"

"Nothin'. Just hanging out," I answered.

"Man I'm starved!" he said.

"Do you want me to make you something?"

"I don't know what I feel like."

I thought for a moment. "How about a grilled cheese?"

"Yeah! That sounds great. Can you make me two?"

"Sure."

"Thanks, Jo. I really appreciate it. You're the best."

"No problem." I got up from the table and started to make the sandwiches. As I placed them into the frying pan, I casually asked, "Is James here?"

"Yeah, he's downstairs."

"Is he with anyone?" I wasn't sure if I really wanted to know the answer, but I couldn't help myself. I had to ask.

"Listen, Jo. I know how much you like James, but he really isn't the right guy for you."

"But—"

"No. Listen. He might be nice to you, but he doesn't treat other girls very well at all. He has problems. He can be really mean. You just don't see it."

"That's because he cares about me."

"I'm sure he does. It's just not the way you think."

"What do you mean?" I handed the plate to Kevin.

"He thinks of you like a sister."

I didn't like that sound of that. "But I don't want him to think of me that way."

"I know. I'm sorry, Jo, but it's really for the best. He isn't good enough for you. You are smart and attractive and you deserve a decent guy who will treat you right."

I was hurt. I knew Kevin was just trying to protect me, but he didn't understand. *I love James. It's not just a little crush. I've loved him since I was ten years old.* "Well if he's such a jerk, why is he your best friend?"

"I'm a guy. It's different with guys. Besides, if he ever treated you mean, like I see him treating other girls, he knows I would beat the shit out of him."

"You think he's just being nice to me because he doesn't want you to beat him up?" I was crushed.

"I don't mean it that way, Jo. He's just not right for you. He's a good guy as a friend, but he wouldn't make a good boyfriend. Especially not for you. You deserve the best. Do you understand what I'm saying?"

"I guess so," I said quietly.

Kevin was wrong. I knew James was a big, tough guy that got into a lot of fights. And I knew he could be mean to people he didn't like. But I also knew that if James fell in love with me, it would be different. He would treat me differently. He just didn't love any of those other girls he'd been with. But I understood why Kevin wanted to protect me. He was just looking out for me. He didn't want me to get hurt. I reached over and took a swig of Kevin's beer.

"Can I have a sip, too?" asked Diana.

"Sure. You two can finish it." He stood up from the table, stretched and rubbed his flat belly. "That was great. It really hit the spot. Thanks a lot, Jo."

"No problem."

"See ya later, guys," he said, and he went back downstairs.

"See ya!" we sang out.

I quickly put the conversation with Kevin out of my head. Kevin and I were really close and he was just being a big brother. He just didn't know the side of James that I knew. The kind, gentle side that he saved for people he cared about.

By the end of the evening, Diana and I had drunk so many sips of everyone's beers that we were feeling pretty happy. I'd gotten three kisses from James, and the last one had been a really long one. Diana had gotten several kisses from a few different guys. We were having a great time.

But best of all, I found out that James had moved in with us!

He'd gotten into a big fight with his father the night before. Then his dad had kicked him out of the house and my mom had agreed to let him stay with us for a little while. *Maybe that's why Kevin tried to convince me to let go of my love for James?*

This is going to be an amazing summer. I'll be able to see him all the time. And the more I see him, the better chance there is that he'll start to like me more. Maybe he'll even start to love me. And if that happens, maybe we could start going around together. If he really loved me, he could maybe talk Kevin into letting him be my boyfriend.

The following weekend, my mom was at Grandma's cottage again. Diana and I were in our usual spots at the kitchen table. James and his friend Pete were down in the basement. My brothers were out somewhere with other friends. Diana thought Pete was a real hunk, and we were both talking about how great it would be to hang out with the two of them.

A little while later, James came up to use the bathroom.

"Hi James," we both sang out.

"Hi, Jo. Hi, Diana. What're you girls up to?"

"Nothin' much. Just hangin' out," I said, trying to sound as casual as I could.

"Can I have a sip of your beer?" Diana asked.

"Sure. You want a whole one?"

I couldn't believe it. This was great! "Can I have one too?" I asked.

"Sure. They're down in the fridge. Go help yourselves." And off he went to the washroom.

Well, we didn't have to be offered twice. We jumped up from the table and ran downstairs to get our beers.

"Hi, Pete," we both called out as we went over to the fridge in the rec room.

"Hey, there."

"James said we could have a beer," I added.

"No problem. Grab me one too, will ya?"

"Here ya go," I said, and held it out for him.

As we started to leave the rec room, Pete asked us where we were going.

"We were just going back to the kitchen," Diana answered.

"Why don't you stay here with us?"

I couldn't believe it. He was actually inviting us to hang out with them.

But then I hesitated. *What if James doesn't want us down here?* I didn't want to do anything to make him mad. I looked over at Diana.

"It's okay," he said.

Just then, James came back in the room and grabbed another beer.

"Have a seat, Jo," he said as he sat down on the bed.

Is this really happening? It was just like all those dreams I'd had, where James would treat me like his girlfriend.

"Yeah, Diana. Why don't you have a seat here?" Pete suggested as he patted a spot beside him on the couch.

Diana quickly sat down by Pete. And I sat down beside James. I was starting to feel nervous. *What should I say?* I didn't want to sound like an idiot. Or even worse, like a little kid.

So I took a swig of my beer to avoid the awkward silence.

Fortunately, Diana was never at a loss for words. She got the conversation going and before long, we were all gabbing and laughing and having a great time. And once I had gulped down a couple of beers, I started to feel braver. By the fourth beer, I was just as outgoing and talkative as Diana.

A little while later, Pete starting kissing Diana. And as they got into heavy necking, I started to feel nervous again. Suddenly, it was just me and James having a conversation. I took another swig of my beer and tried to act as casual as possible.

What should I say to him? As I stared into his beautiful face, I wanted so badly to kiss him. But I was afraid to. What if he didn't want me to? What if he got mad and sent me upstairs? Then I looked over at Diana and Pete. They were now lying down on the couch, still necking.

I found myself staring at them, to avoid having to think of something clever to say to James. And as I stared, I took another gulp of beer. I was so focused on Diana and Pete that I didn't notice that James had moved closer to me. But then I felt him touch my shoulder and pull me in toward him. And he kissed me. I was in heaven. I melted into his arms as he held me close and continued to kiss me. I could tell by the way he was necking that he was getting really excited. And then I heard him moan. *Or was that me?*

As we continued to kiss, I realized that someone had shut out the lights. Then James pulled me down into a lying position on the bed. I still couldn't believe this was happening. It was everything I had always dreamed it would be. *He does love me. He has to. He would never kiss me this way if he didn't love me.* My excitement was building and I could feel his excitement pressing up against me.

This is it. He's going to make love to me. I want him to. I want to show him how much I love him. I've always wanted him to be my first.

And then I thought about Carl. I remembered that conversation we had, a long time ago. It had to be at least a year ago now. He said he would be so disappointed in me if I lost my virginity before I was old enough.

And then I thought about the time I was with that guy. The one that Diana's boyfriend had brought with him. His name was Dave.

We'd been kissing and Dave was trying to undo my pants. I didn't want him to get mad at me for stopping him. But then I thought about what Carl had said, and suddenly I didn't care if he got mad. I wasn't going to let him take my virginity. So I stopped him. And I was right. He'd gotten really pissed off at me and accused me of being a tease. But I didn't care. I had been so thankful that Carl's words had given me the strength to stop him.

As James continued to kiss me, I felt him undo my pants. And then I thought about Carl again. But this time it was different. Carl was gone. He had left and I'd never heard from him again. He'd only pretended to love me. He didn't care about me at all.

But James loves me. And I love him. This is my big chance to prove it to James. To prove to him just how much I really do love him. This will bond us together forever. He will always be my first. He will always be the one who took my virginity. Then he will have to admit that he loves me, too.

As we continued kissing, he removed my pants as well as his own. I spread my legs as he positioned himself over top of me.

This is it. It's really happening.

And then he plunged himself into me with such force.

I instantly screamed out in agonizing pain. I didn't mean to, but the pain was so severe I couldn't help myself.

James immediately stopped. He propped himself up on extended arms and said, "Fuck!" as he took a deep breath and rolled off of me.

As I lay there waiting for the pain to subside, I realized that James hadn't known that I was a virgin. *How could he not know? Did he think I was a slut? Did he think I would let just anybody be my first? He had to know that I would let only him do this to me. He had to know that my love for him was that strong.*

He had rolled over to face the wall and as I continued to silently lie there, I felt the blood pooling underneath me.

I quietly got up from the bed, grabbed my pants and tiptoed out of the room.

The following day, Diana and I were sitting out on the bench on my driveway, watching James fix his motorcycle further down at the bottom of the drive.

I stared at him and sighed.

"Just think of it," Diana whispered. "That hunk down there balled you last night!"

No. He made love to me. I didn't correct her. "I know. I still can't believe it." Then I sighed again at the thought of it.

James hadn't said a word to us. He acted as though it had never happened. But it had happened, and he could never change that.

Two days later, when I came in for supper, my mom was standing there in the kitchen, as if she'd been waiting for me.

"You're grounded, you little slut!" she screamed.

"What're you talking about?"

"I know what that James boy did to you."

"He didn't do anything." *How could she possibly know? She couldn't. The only people that knew were Diana, Pete and James. And I know that they wouldn't say anything.*

"Don't deny it. I know you aren't a virgin anymore. And I know it was that James who did it."

She couldn't possibly know. She had to be guessing. But what would make her even think it? "I have no idea what you're talking about. I didn't do anything. And you're wrong. I am so still a virgin. How could you even think such a thing?"

Then she posed herself in a mocking way and started to recite, "I love James so much. And he made love to me last night! I gave my virginity to him."

I realized immediately what she had done. I was livid. "How dare you!"

"Don't you speak to me that way."

"You had no right to read my diary."

I could see a slight twinge of guilt as her face turned red.

But she quickly recovered. "That's not the point. And, you might as well know, I've kicked him out. How dare he screw you, under my own roof. And after I felt sorry for him and took him in."

Oh no. How could she do such a thing? Where is he going to go now? "He didn't do anything to me."

"You liar. You wouldn't have written it in your diary if it wasn't true."

"Well that's how much you know. It wasn't true. I just wanted it to be true."

"I don't believe you. And even if you're right, I don't want him in my house."

I thought about my diary again. "I hate you!" I ran up to my room and slammed the door. I had always been so careful to lock my diary and hide it. I didn't trust her. I knew she would read it if she had the chance. *She's so damn nosy.* But the night before, I hadn't bothered to lock it. And I hadn't taken the time to hide it all that well, either. I'd just shoved it into the top drawer of my dresser.

I pulled out my diary and started to read over some of my most recent entries. And as I did, I got more and more angry. To think she'd read all my most private thoughts. *I hate her. How could she invade my privacy this way?*

At first, I decided it was the last time I was going to ever write in my diary again. And then I had an idea. I started to write all about how much I hated her, and about how I had lied about James. How I hadn't lost my virginity at all. *That'll show her. It will serve her right, the next time she goes snooping.*

I was sure that there would be a next time. She couldn't help herself. And I was right. A few weeks later, she brought up something else I'd purposely written in my diary for her benefit. We had a huge fight about it, but I was secretly pleased she'd read all the nasty things I wrote about her.

Little did she know I had started to use one of my school notebooks as my new diary. It was actually a lot better. I had so much more room to write. And I'd become very careful to hide it well, even though I knew she would never suspect it was anything more than an old school notebook.

It was several months later before we had another fight about my privacy. My mom had sent Kevin away to Ireland to live with the old man, because of all the trouble he was getting into. She'd said she couldn't handle him anymore and that it was for his own good. *Liar. She just wanted to get rid of him.*

At first he didn't want to go, but then he decided it would be an adventure. We had agreed to write each other every week, but it took so long for my letters to get over there and for his to come back that we ended up writing only every few weeks.

Kevin and I had always been close and, initially, I was afraid we would grow apart because he was so far away. But instead, we actually became even closer. I would tell him all about what was going on in my life and he would fill me in on what it was like for him over there.

Then one day, I came home from school and my mom announced that another letter had come from Kevin. I flew up the stairs with excitement.

My mom held the envelope out to me and I instantly freaked. "You opened it."

"Of course I opened it."

I couldn't believe she would stoop so low. *How dare she open a letter that was addressed to me.* I screamed and yelled and threatened to call the police on her. "It's against the law to open someone's mail."

"It's my house and he's my son. I have every right to open any mail that comes into this house."

I grabbed the letter out of her hand and ran to the stairs, shouting, "I hate your guts. And I'm going to tell Kevin that you're opening his letters."

When I got to my room, I quickly scanned his letter and was relieved to discover that he hadn't said anything that revealed any of the things I had written in my last letter to him. He had referred to some of them, but I knew she wouldn't be able to figure out what he was talking about. *That's good. Let her wonder.*

Later that night, when I was trying to fall asleep, I couldn't stop thinking about what she had done. I was still so furious. I knew I would never get to sleep unless I put it out of my head. So I took a few deep breaths to relax.

Hello, luv.

William! I'm so glad you're here. And I was glad. It had been quite some time since we had visited. I had become so busy when I wasn't at home, and when I was home, I spent most of my time fighting with my mom. And I missed William. They always made me feel so much better about myself. And my life.

We are with you always. You know that.

Yes, but we haven't talked in such a long time.

And on what topic do you wish to speak?

I thought about my mom reading my letter. And I thought about when she read my diary. *Why won't my mother respect my privacy?*

Let us ask you something. Do you expect your mother to give you privacy?

I thought about it and I had to admit that I didn't.

That is your answer.

I wasn't exactly sure what they meant. *Are you saying it's my fault that she read my diary? And my letter?*

There is no blame, dear one.

But I want my privacy. Why won't she leave my things alone?

Let us ask you another question. How did you feel when you hid this diary?

I was afraid. I figured she would snoop and I was right.

Your thoughts created this. And your fears brought it into your reality.

We'd had this kind of discussion before, and I was finally starting to understand what they meant. *So you're saying that no matter what I think about, it will happen?*

When you think a great deal on a subject and your focus is strong and your expectations are even stronger, it will be. It must be.

But I didn't want it. I thought that only happened when I really wanted something.

You must pay very close attention to how you are feeling.

What do you mean?

Your feelings will tell you whether it is something you want that is being created. Or something that you do not want.

As I thought about this for a moment, I started to get nervous. I started to think about the times when I had thought about unpleasant things. And then I started to feel scared.

Do not be frightened, dear child.

But I do think about bad things. Does that mean that all those negative things are going to happen?

Only if you think about them a great deal of the time. And only if you feel very strongly about the subject. And then, only if you truly believe that it will happen.

That made me feel a little better. I didn't always think about negative things. I thought about good things a lot, too. But it did make me realize that I was going to have to pay much greater attention to my thoughts from now on. And my feelings.

You are really learning well. We are pleased.

And as they said it, I could feel their pleasure. And I was pleased with myself, too. And as my pleasure grew stronger and stronger, I felt that familiar love and joy wash over me. I loved the way William made me feel. I felt strong and beautiful and loved.

I love you so much William, I sang out in my mind. And I felt their love grow even stronger, if that was even possible.

Our love for you is greater than you know.

Chapter 19

Over the next year, Diana went steady with a number of different boys. And, as usual, I was the third wheel. Then one Friday night, her latest boyfriend Brian brought along a friend named Gary. He was fairly good-looking, so I wasn't surprised when Brian told me he wasn't interested in me. But it still hurt. *Why does it always have to be this way? Why does Diana always get the guy she likes and I never do? Why can't I just be satisfied with the ones that aren't so good-looking?*

And then I remembered. This was a conversation I had with myself over and over. And then I reminded myself of the conclusion I had come to a while back. I was riding on the bus one day, when a young couple caught my eye. They weren't very attractive. She was short and dumpy, with a big round face and small inset eyes. The skin on her cheeks had large pockmarks, and when she smiled, I could see her crooked, yellow teeth. He was tall and skinny, with a long boney face and a bad case of acne. He wore big, fat, rimmed glasses that seemed to take over his entire face.

I couldn't take my eyes off of them. But they were totally oblivious to my staring. In fact, they seemed oblivious to everything around them. That's what had intrigued me so much. As I secretly watched them, I saw her gaze up into his eyes with the most adoring look on her face. And as his eyes stared back into hers, he reached out and gently took her hand. He leaned over and gave her a loving kiss on the mouth. And they smiled at each other.

I found myself smiling at their warm, loving exchange. And as I finally looked away, I wondered how they each couldn't see that the other wasn't very attractive. The way they gazed at each other, it was clear they each thought they were looking at the most beautiful person in the world. *Why can't someone look at me that way?*

And then I realized that wasn't really the problem. The problem was that the only guys that found me attractive were the ones that I didn't find attractive. And as I thought about this further, I realized that my real problem was my taste in boys. I always found myself attracted to the best looking guys. *But I am not very good-*

looking. So why can't I be attracted to the ones that aren't very attractive? Why can't I be like the couple on the bus?

They obviously knew they weren't very attractive, so they were able to gravitate to each other and love each other. And see the inner beauty in each other.

Why can't I do that? It's not like I haven't tried. I have. But I just can't seem to feel attracted to someone who isn't good-looking. It's a flaw in my character. I can't seem to match my attraction to someone with similar looks to my own.

And there it was. I had finally figured it out. The problem was that I thought like a pretty person. My mom had always told me how beautiful I was. All her adult friends used to say how beautiful I was. And Carl had always told me that, too. He used to say I was going to break a lot of boys' hearts when I got older. Even William always told me how beautiful I was.

It's their fault I think the way I do. They convinced me that I was beautiful, but the reality is that I'm not. And now my brain is wired wrong. Now when I look at a guy, I see him through the eyes of someone who thinks she can actually attract a good-looking person. Until I look in the mirror, that is. Then I am reminded of what I really look like. Or until I let a good-looking guy know how I feel, and then he reminds me of what I really look like.

As I remembered back to that day on the bus, I got angry again. *How could they do this to me? How could they set me up for a life of disappointment? I'm sure they didn't mean to. They probably thought they were doing me a favour. Some favour!*

"Hey, Jo. What's up?" I heard Diana saying.

"Nothing. I was just thinking."

"Thinking about what?"

"Nothing."

"Why don't you go and talk to Gary?" she whispered.

I sighed. *Here we go again.* "I don't know. I don't think he likes me."

"What makes you think that?"

Because he's good-looking and I'm ugly, that's why. "I just don't."

"Well you could be wrong. He seems nice. Why don't you give it a shot?"

I could tell she was trying to get rid of me. She wanted to make out with Brian and she wanted me to keep Gary busy. So I went over to where Gary was sitting and tried to start a conversation. But he wasn't being very talkative. In fact, as I started to talk to him, I could tell he didn't have much to say at all. I wasn't sure whether it was because he was a bit of a drip or because he just didn't like me and couldn't be bothered to make the effort to talk to me.

Then he offered me a beer and I took it thankfully. *Maybe once we've had a few beers it won't be so awkward. Otherwise, this is going to be a long night.*

And I was right. After we had drunk three beers each, I loosened up and started to talk more easily. And he started to talk a little more, too. That's when I realized he actually was a bit of a drip. He seemed to have no sense of humour whatsoever. And as if that wasn't bad enough, he just didn't seem to have anything interesting to say.

But the beers were starting to make me feel good, so I didn't really care. At least he was nice to look at. We were both on our fourth beer when he leaned in and kissed me. It was dry and he lacked enthusiasm. And then I realized I wasn't all that into him, either. *Good-looking or not, he's a bore. And a lousy kisser, on top of it.*

A short time earlier, Diana and Brian had disappeared into a bedroom to make out. So now we were stuck with each other. *God, I hate this!* But as I started to feel the effects of the booze, he started to seem more and more interesting to me. *And besides, I should be thankful that he's even interested in me.*

So before I knew it, we were making out heavily, and next thing I knew we were having sex. It was over in a matter of minutes. And it was awful.

I got up and put my clothes back on, grabbed my purse and headed for the door. I couldn't bear the thought of having to make conversation with him. "Tell Diana I had to go home. I'll talk to her tomorrow." And I left.

As I walked home, I started to feel worse and worse. *Why did I let him do that to me?* I didn't even really like him. I felt so dirty— so cheap. *But he must have liked me. Otherwise, why would he want to have sex with me? I should be thankful that a good-looking guy had wanted to be with me. He probably didn't really like me. I just happened to be the only one available at the time.*

It was exactly two weeks later, to the day, when I saw him the next time. I had decided not to go out with Diana and Brian that night. I couldn't get to sleep the night before and I felt really tired. I just wanted to crawl into bed early with a good book.

And that's exactly what I was doing when he showed up at my house at around ten o'clock that night. I had recently taken over the rec room as my bedroom, now that my brothers weren't living at home. And because they had only just moved out, I assumed it was one of my brothers' friends when I heard the knock on the door.

So there I was, standing in my comfy granny gown pyjamas, staring at Gary. *What the hell is he doing here? And how does he even know where I live?* He was the last person I wanted to see. But there he was, all smiles and clearly drunk. Not fall-down drunk, but I could tell he'd been drinking.

"Aren't you going to invite me in?"

"I guess. Come on in."

I walked up to the kitchen and he followed. *Maybe if I don't encourage him, he'll realize I'm not interested and just leave.*

No such luck. He was actually making quite an effort to carry on a conversation. And I wasn't giving him much to work with. He was being extra friendly and I just wasn't into it. *Why doesn't he take the hint and leave?*

"Are you the only one home?"

I was. My mom had taken my little sister with her to my grandma's cottage, and Carol was staying over at a friend's place.

"Yeah, but my mom should be home soon."

"So where's your bedroom?"

Is he just making small talk? Or does he have a reason for asking?

"Downstairs."

"Why don't we go downstairs then?"

Well that answered that. I knew exactly what he was getting at. It was the last thing I felt like doing, but then I remembered the last time. *If I just give it to him, maybe he'll leave and I can get some sleep. But why should I? I don't want it, so why should I just give in? And why does he even want me? Look at me. I am a mess. I know I'm not attractive at the best of times, but right now, I look awful. Maybe he does like me after all? Finally, a good-looking guy is attracted to me, and I don't even like him. Well isn't this just great.*

"Come on. Let's go downstairs."

He got up and headed toward the stairs, so I followed.

I knew what he was after and I was right. The minute we got to my room, he grabbed my hand and led me to the bed. He quickly took off his pants and pulled my nightgown up.

"I'm not in the mood," I groaned feebly.

"Ah, come on. Sure you are."

I thought I caught a tone in his voice. What was it? Annoyance? Or did he sound insulted? I couldn't tell for sure. And if he was insulted, why? Was he insulted that someone like me would turn him down? That someone like me should feel lucky that he wanted to be with her?

And then it was over. He was finished. He quickly got up and rushed to put his pants back on. "I better get going before your mom gets home."

I made no effort to correct him.

And as I heard the door slam shut upstairs, it suddenly occurred to me that he hadn't even kissed me. All I could think about was how relieved I was that he was finally gone. *But how could I have let him use me that way? I'm becoming a slut. All because I'm so ugly. If I was pretty, this would never have happened. If I was pretty, I could pick who I wanted to be with. I wouldn't have to be stuck with someone just because he wanted me. Or just because he wanted to use me.*

I felt the tears flowing down my face and didn't even bother to wipe them away. *Why am I so ugly? It isn't fair. Why can't I be pretty, like Diana? Why can't I have a boyfriend? One that I care about? One that likes me back?* I felt so alone. So unloved. So worthless. And as the tears flowed, I finally drifted off to sleep.

*

Over the next couple of days, I started to notice that something had changed. I had changed. I knew I was feeling depressed, but it was something more than that. And then on Monday, I came on my period. That was when I realized I'd been afraid I might be pregnant.

And for half the day I felt relieved. But when my period ended as quickly as it had started, my feelings instantly changed from relief to panic.

Now I was sure I must be pregnant. I could feel it. I just knew I was. But I didn't say anything to anyone. Not even Diana. It was too soon. I had to be certain. I would have to wait to see if I came on my period the next month.

I couldn't believe how slowly the days went by. It felt as though time was standing still. Then two weeks later, my drama teacher gave us a large project to work on. *Finally, something to keep me busy while I impatiently wait!*

We were all assigned to small groups to put on a play. The teacher said we could either pick an existing play or write one of our own. He said we would get bonus marks if we wrote our own. I was matched up with two rich girls, Cheryl and Monica. I didn't really know them all that well. They hung around a totally different crowd from me.

While they were busy trying to find an existing play, I started to write my own. And then a week later, they said how frustrated they were that they still hadn't found one they liked.

"That's okay. I've written one myself."

"You have? When?"

"I finished it last night." Then I handed the play over to Monica.

I started to feel nervous as I waited for them to read through it. *What if they don't like it? What if they refuse to use it? God, it's taking them forever to read it!*

But eventually, when Cheryl had finally finished, she looked over at Monica and then at me.

"This is good," she said.

She sounded surprised. I had decided that I was going to take the character who didn't talk through the whole thing. I figured that if I gave each of them the big speaking parts, they might be more inclined to agree to use my play. And besides, I wanted to be the director, so it would be easier if I didn't have to say any lines. I told them that they could pick between the two speaking parts and I would take the part of Katie.

They both seemed pleased.

We arranged to get together on Sunday at Monica's house to practice.

When I arrived at her house, I hesitated before walking up the driveway. Her house was so much bigger than mine and I felt a little nervous about going inside. It wasn't just the house. I was nervous about working with the two of them on this project. None of my friends were rich and I had never known anyone that was.

What if they don't like me? What if they know I'm poor? What if they treat me differently because my family doesn't have any money? I took a deep breath and walked up the driveway.

Once we got settled into Monica's bedroom, I started to relax. I just focused on the play and started to explain to them how I envisioned it being acted. They stood there silently and listened.

I couldn't believe it! They were actually listening to me. "So why don't we get started?" I suggested.

Cheryl had the first line. She was awful.

"That was good, Cheryl. But try to remember, your character has a secret."

I proceeded to explain to her, again, what was really going on in her character's mind.

"Then why does she say what she does?"

"Because she doesn't want her friend to know what she's thinking. She's trying to hide her secret," I explained. Again! And so it went, back and forth like that all morning.

"Okay. Why don't we take a lunch break?" I suggested.

Monica and Cheryl went downstairs to make themselves some lunch, and I pulled out my sandwich from my purse and started to eat it. While they were gone, I took the opportunity to look around her room. It was twice the size of my room, even considering that I was now using our rec room as my bedroom.

As I studied it carefully, I noticed that it still looked like a little girls' room. I had to admit, though, that I would have been really envious if I had seen this room back when I was younger.

I had already finished my sandwich by the time they came back to the room with their lunch. I pulled out a couple of cookies I'd packed and started to slowly eat them. I was feeling uncomfortable now that we were no longer working on the play. I didn't know what to say to them. I didn't even know whether they actually expected me to say anything.

As I listened to them talking and giggling like little kids, I couldn't help thinking about the possibility that I might be pregnant. I suddenly became embarrassed and forced myself to stop thinking about it.

You idiot. You act as though they can read your mind. They have no idea. Listen to them. Not a care in the world. And look at Monica. She's going on and on about her new pair of underpants. Goddamn underpants! Can you believe it? Here I am, worried about being pregnant and she's talking about her new underpants.

A short while later, we were back rehearsing and I was back directing. I put everything else out of my mind and concentrated on the play. By the end of the day, their acting was slowly starting to get better. Not great, but definitely better.

We agreed to meet again on Tuesday after school to continue rehearsing, and then again the next Sunday. And that's how it went over the next several weeks.

I finally told Diana about my fear of being pregnant as we were walking into our next class. I hadn't come on my period ever since that one half-day period two months earlier. I was pretty certain I really was pregnant, but I hadn't actually had it confirmed by a test yet.

"So what do you think?" I whispered, as we took our seats.

"What do you mean?"

"Do you think I'm pregnant?"

"Well. I suppose it's possible. But not probable."

What the hell does she mean by that? It's possible but not probable? That doesn't make any sense. I had sex without using any birth control and I haven't had a period in two months. Is she an idiot? No she's probably just scared. She just doesn't want to believe it. She doesn't want it to be true, so she's acting as though it's not likely.

After class, Diana talked me into going to see the guidance counsellor. At first I said no, but then I finally agreed to. I got the feeling she was just trying to pass the buck. She didn't know how to deal with it, so she passed the responsibility on to someone else. I didn't blame her, though. I didn't know how to deal with it either. I was scared. No—I was terrified.

The truth was, I was most afraid of telling my mom. Oh, I didn't think she would freak out over the pregnancy, but I knew she would insist that I have an abortion. I had given it a lot of thought and decided I couldn't do it. I wanted to have the baby and give it up for adoption. And that's what she would freak out over!

I explained everything to the counsellor and she said there were a number of ways I could handle the situation, including dealing with my mom. First of all, I needed to get tested to confirm that I really was pregnant. She said she would make an appointment for me right away with the family planning clinic. Then she said I could just hold off telling my mom until after the deadline for having an abortion had past.

"I couldn't do that," I told her. *That would be worse. My mom would never forgive me. She might even kick me out of the house. Then what would I do?*

Then she offered to go with me to tell my mom. That was a good idea. Mom would never freak out in front of the guidance counsellor. Would she? It was definitely less likely than if I was alone.

So it was all set. She would let me know the date of my appointment tomorrow and, depending on how it went, she would come home with me to tell my mom.

The next day I found out I had one more week of not knowing for sure and then it would be official. Then I would be officially pregnant. I had become more and more sure of it as time went by and I still hadn't come on my period.

The only problem was, my appointment was the same day we were scheduled to put on my play. My drama class was second period of the day and I was going to have to skip my last period to make it to the clinic on time.

Diana had agreed to come with me, so that was a relief. But I was having such a hard time concentrating on anything. *Maybe it's a blessing that my play is the same day. It'll help to distract me. I hope.*

When the day finally arrived, I was a basket case! I was so nervous about the play and even more nervous about the pregnancy test. My mind kept flipping back and forth between the two. How was I ever going to survive the day?

As the three of us walked up onto the stage, I could barely breathe. I could feel my heart pounding in my chest and suddenly I was so glad I didn't have any lines. I didn't think I could speak.

And then I thought about Monica and Cheryl. *What if they forget their lines? What if they screw up and say their lines wrong?* They had come a long way in the last several weeks and I'd been pleased with our final rehearsal on Sunday. But what if they were just as nervous as me?

As the lights went down over my classmates in the audience, I put everything else out of my mind and focused on my part in the play. And when we were done, I suddenly started to panic again.

There was a huge silence.

They hated it. Our teacher hated it. I thought it had gone well, but I must be wrong.

Suddenly, I heard a bellowing sound as my teacher came storming up the stage stairs, clapping his hands and shouting, "Excellent! Simply superb! A-plus! A-plus-plus!"

I couldn't believe my ears. Here was my quiet drama teacher showing such enthusiasm. The same teacher I had come to believe really hated his job. He always had this disappointed air about him. But now he sounded excited. He liked it. He really, really liked it.

But then I started to worry that Monica and Cheryl would get all the credit. After all, they had the speaking parts. The actors always got all the credit. And even though my part was actually very difficult, I didn't have any lines. So they might not realize how hard it was to act without the benefit of any lines.

But the teacher knew I had written and directed it. He had to know the extent of my efforts. He's a drama teacher, for God's sake. He must know what it takes to write and direct and act in a play.

And then I noticed the silence in the audience again. The lights on the stage were blinding and it was still dark out in the audience, so I couldn't see my classmates.

Oh no. They hated it. Or worse, they didn't get it.

But as the lights came back on, I was stunned to see that they were all standing up and clapping. And cheering.

I was in a daze. I couldn't believe what I was seeing. And hearing. And then I looked over at Monica and Cheryl. And they were standing there looking at me and clapping too. *The clapping was all being directed at me.*

I took a deep breath and tried to control my tears.

Later that day, as Diana and I walked over to the clinic, I told her all about what had happened that morning in drama class. I wanted to savour my feelings about the success of my play. And I didn't want to think about where we going. Or why.

As I sat in the waiting room, I started to think about what other explanation there could be for not having a period. And then it occurred to me that I might be seriously ill. That maybe I had some terminal disease. *What if I'm dying?* And the terror gripped me. I couldn't breathe. All of a sudden, being pregnant didn't seem that bad.

So when they told me I was in fact pregnant, there was this moment when I felt relieved. But only a moment. Then I thought about my mom. And the terror returned. *How can I possibly tell her?*

A week later, I did just that. And it was just as I had expected. My mom freaked out when the counsellor told her I didn't want to have an abortion. At first, she tried to persuade me to change my mind. Then finally, she announced that she would make me have an abortion.

As it turned out, I had no rights at all. I wasn't sixteen yet, so my mom held all the cards. She could insist that I have an abortion and there was nothing I could do about it. The counsellor told me later that I could continue to tell the doctors that I didn't want it, right up to the moment they were about to start the operation, and that maybe they would refuse to continue, but I was too afraid to do that.

So instead, I went along with it in the end. She had gotten her way and I was the one who had to live with the guilt.

Chapter 20

In the months that followed, I kept mainly to myself. I didn't even spend much time with Diana. She was busy hanging out with her latest boyfriend, and I just couldn't bear the thought of being the same old third wheel. We still talked on the phone, and I still saw her at school, but I just wasn't into socializing. *She doesn't understand how I'm feeling. How could she? She hasn't gone through what I have.*

It was late spring when I finally started feeling a little better. At least I was able to get through a day without thinking about what I had done. About what my mom had made me do. The depression and guilt eventually led to anger—anger at myself for getting pregnant in the first place and anger at my mom for making me have an abortion.

So when Diana asked me if I wanted to go to the drive-in movie with her and her new boyfriend Tony, I said yes. I needed to get out of the house. I needed a change. I wanted to feel happy again.

When we got to Tony's apartment and I realized that his friend Adam was coming to the drive-in with us, I was pissed off. *Oh God. What the hell was she thinking? How could she do this to me? Again!*

But then I decided to make the best of it. *It's just a movie, after all. I'm not interested in him and I don't have to do anything I don't want to do.* So off we went.

Tony and Diana sat in the front seat of Tony's van and Adam and I sat in the back. We were on our third beer when I realized that Adam didn't seem so bad after all. At least he wasn't a total idiot. We could actually have a decent conversation. *Not like that jerk, Gary.*

No. Don't even think about it.

So when we finished our fourth beer and Adam leaned over and kissed me, I didn't really mind. I kissed him back. And for the next couple of hours, I never did see the movie. Instead, we drank beer and talked and kissed. And it was quite pleasant. I was feeling pretty good. As it turned out, I was glad I'd come after all.

When the movie was over, we drove back to Tony's place. The beer had run out a while back, and I was starting to feel a little mellow, so I decided to rest my eyes on the way back to Tony's.

They woke me up when we got there, and then all I wanted to do was go home to bed. But Diana had other plans. She wanted to make out with Tony, so I was stuck waiting for her. She promised that Tony would drive us home after. She said I had to wait only maybe an hour.

But now that I had sobered up, I realized I really wasn't attracted to Adam, and I didn't even want to make the effort to make small talk with him.

What if he wants to continue where we left off at the drive-in? Just the thought of it made me feel sick. *How could I even think he was attractive? I just want to go to sleep.*

So I curled up on the arm chair and started to doze. I don't know how much time had gone by, but as I started to wake up, I realized that Adam was on top of me. He was trying to kiss me, and his hands were moving all over my body.

I instantly froze. "No!" I shouted, and I tried to push his hands off of me.

"What do you mean, no?" he said.

He sounded scary. *What is he doing? He isn't listening to me.* "Stop it. I don't want this."

"You wanted it earlier. You can't just shut it off. You want it. You know you do." Somehow he had managed to get my pants undone and he had his hand inside them.

I tried to kick, but he had my legs pinned down.

He was forcing his fingers inside me and he had this frightening look on his face.

I was terrified. I kept squirming and trying to break free of his hold. But I couldn't. "Help!" I screamed.

"Shut up, you bitch."

"Let me go," I demanded as loud as I could. But the harder I fought him, the more determined he got. "Diana! Help me. Please," I pleaded. *She had to hear me. She's only in the next room. Why isn't she coming?*

And then my anger took over. And my fear. *He's going to rape me!* I starting kicking and punching and screaming.

He kept holding me down with his arms and legs and the rest of his body. And I felt the pain, as he plunged his fingers into me harder and harder.

But I kept fighting. I had to. I was fighting for my life! *He has no right to do this. He's hurting me. I have to get away.* And I screamed and screamed and kicked and punched. I was in a frenzy. I don't know exactly when, or how, but somehow I suddenly broke free. I stumbled to the door, trying to pull up my pants, as I scrambled to get out. But he was right behind me.

The minute I was out the door, I screamed at the top of my lungs. "Help! Please help me!"

He's coming after me. But just as I saw a lady come out of one of the apartments down the hall, I heard the door behind me slam shut. Then I ran the rest of the way down the hall. I fell into her arms, sobbing, as I quickly looked back to make sure he wasn't still there.

I don't remember all the details of the next twelve hours. I know that the police came. I know I was taken to the hospital and I know that they examined me. I don't remember how I got back home. I think they gave me something to calm me down at the hospital, so maybe that's why I can't remember the details.

What I do remember is the fear. I remember my whole body trembling. And then it would jerk uncontrollably. I knew he was nowhere near me, but I couldn't shake the fear. When I awoke in my own bed, late the following morning, I immediately thought about what had happened the night before.

As it played over in my mind like a horrible nightmare, the fear gripped me again. I knew it wasn't just a bad dream. I knew it was real. And I knew it was all my fault. *I should never have gone in the first place. I should never have drunk those beers. But worst of all, I should never have kissed him. How could I be so stupid?* Just the thought of it made me feel sick. I tried not to think about the details of what he did. But I couldn't help myself. It kept playing over and over in my mind.

And then I thought about Diana. *Why didn't she come and help me? I was screaming at the top of my lungs. But she never came. I called out to her. But she didn't come to help. How could she ignore me that way? How could she let this happen? She's supposed to be my best friend.*

I buried myself in my room that day. I didn't want to talk to anyone. I was too ashamed. *How could I let this happen?* I hadn't talked to my mom about it yet either. I knew she knew what had happened. But thankfully, she left me alone. I didn't want to hear her blaming me. I didn't want to hear the words said out loud.

And then I got angry. I thought about what he had done. *It wasn't just my fault. I have the right to say no. Even if I did kiss him earlier. I have the right to change my mind. He had no right to force himself on me. He had no right to hurt me that way.* It was strange, but the anger actually made me feel better. Stronger.

As the day went on, I started to think that the worst of it was behind me, until two detectives showed up later that afternoon. As I walked in the living room, I felt the fear grip me instantly, along with the guilt and the shame.

I sat with my mom on the couch and each of the detectives sat in the corner chairs across from us. The older one asked all the questions, while the other one just sat and listened and wrote in his book. He made me relive it all.

I admitted that I had been drinking beer. And I admitted that I had kissed him at the drive-in. And eventually, after he asked dozens of questions, the whole story came out. Every horrible detail.

"You said you called out to your friend?" He flipped back in his book. "Diana, is it?"

"Yes."

"Why do you suppose she didn't come to your aid?"

He doesn't believe me! I knew why. I'd figured it out earlier. It was because she was making out with Tony and she just couldn't be bothered. She was probably right in the middle of having sex and that's all that mattered to her. "I don't know," I answered quietly.

"What was she doing in the bedroom?"

Having sex. What do you think? "I don't know."

"Diana says she was in the back room talking to her boyfriend."

Talking, my ass.

"She says she didn't hear you call out to her."

She's a liar. She had to hear me. "I don't understand how she couldn't hear me. I was screaming really loud."

"And you called out her name? And you specifically shouted, help?"

"Yes."

"Why do you suppose she said she didn't hear you?"

They don't believe me. Isn't it obvious? She didn't want to admit she was having sex. "Maybe they had music playing," I offered.

"Do you remember if there was music playing?"

"I'm not sure. I don't remember."

"Now you said he only used his hands to penetrate you. Is that correct?"

Only! What do you mean, only? "Yes."

"Okay. I think we have everything."

"So what happens now?" my mom asked.

"Well, you need to decide whether you want to press charges." He was looking right at me.

"What happens if she does? Do you think we have a case?"

"Well, ma'am. It's clear that there was an assault. He didn't deny it." Then he looked over at me.

"Your story is consistent with what we already have. Except for your girlfriend. And the examination results are consistent with an assault occurring."

He didn't deny it! That has to be good. I thought for sure he would lie.

"I need to warn you, though. These trials can get really ugly. It's usually very hard on the victim. His lawyer will do anything he can to discredit you."

Was he trying to talk me out of pressing charges? But he has to pay for what he did.

"I have an embarrassing question that I need to ask."

And this wasn't embarrassing? All these questions?

"Were you a virgin, before last night?"

Oh no. There it is. None of this counts if I'm not a virgin. Does that mean that anyone can assault someone or rape them, as long as the girl has had sex before? That can't be right. That isn't fair. He assaulted me and he admitted to it. Why can't that be enough?

"No, she's not. She had an incident a while back and she got pregnant. She had an abortion. Will that make a difference?" my mom asked.

"Well, it certainly could. If his lawyer manages to drag it out in court, it could be very difficult for Joanne."

He's going to get away with it. I just know it. Why does it even have to go to trial? He admitted to it.

"But are you saying we should just do nothing? That we should let him get away with it?" I blurted out.

He looked a little embarrassed. "Well he isn't just getting away with it. I have to tell you. When we talked to him last night, he was extremely upset. He kept asking if he was going to lose his job because of this. And I'm sure he's still very frightened right now."

He's upset? He's worried about losing his job! Big bloody deal. He should lose his job. He should be thrown in jail for what he did. This isn't fair.

"I tell you what. What if we wait a couple of days to tell him that you aren't pressing charges? We'll let him sweat for a while. How does that sound?"

Then my mom chimed in. "Do you really want to put yourself through all of this, Joanne? It sounds like he isn't totally getting away with it. And if they leave him to suffer for a couple of days. Let him worry and not know for sure what will happen. What do you think?"

It doesn't matter what I think. They had all made up their minds. I had to admit, though, the way he described what might happen at the trial was frightening. I didn't want to go through that.

I felt defeated. It was as though I was being violated all over again. "Do you promise not to tell him right away?"

"Absolutely. Does this mean that you aren't going to press charges? I need to hear you say it."

What choice do I have? None of you want me to. Not even my mom. "I guess not," I said quietly.

"I think you've made a wise decision."

Then they got up, said their goodbyes, and left.

As I walked back down to my room, my mom kept telling me that this was all for the best. That it would have been a terrible experience if I'd chosen to go through with the trial.

I didn't say anything. I just wanted to be alone.

When I got to my room, I tried to contact William. I took a few deep breaths and tried to relax. "William. I need you," I cried out.

Then the tears came and I started sobbing uncontrollably. I just couldn't stop myself.

And William didn't come.

Chapter 21

Over the next few months, I didn't spend much time with Diana. I was still so upset with her betrayal. Besides, she was spending all her time with Tony and I had no interest in hanging out with the two of them.

When I had asked her why she didn't come and help me when I yelled out to her, she gave me some lame excuse. She said she thought we were having sex and just making a lot of noise. She said she thought I wanted to be with him.

And when I asked her why she lied to the cops, she said she didn't want to tell them that she was having sex and that she thought we were too. I asked her how she could possibly think that my shouting help and pleading for her to come was the kind of thing I would do if I was willingly having sex with him. She said she didn't hear me shouting her name or shouting help.

I didn't believe her.

For the first few weeks after, I couldn't sleep in the basement by myself. I kept trying, but each night I would eventually go upstairs and crawl into bed with my mom. But when she suggested that I move back upstairs to my old room with Shirley, I told her I was okay. I didn't want to give up my privacy, so I decided I was just going to have to get used to sleeping down there again. I spent most of my spare time in my room doing homework, writing in my journal and reading.

The school year was over and Diana had gotten a full-time job for the summer. I didn't have anything to pass the time, so I kept reading and reading and reading. I didn't mind, though. I loved to read. I mostly preferred to read romances and mysteries, but this time I had just finished a really scary book about satanic possession. The part that scared me the most was where the doctors were talking about the power of suggestion. When I read that, it reminded me of what William had taught me. About how, if you think about something enough, you can make it happen.

So when I went to bed that night, it was no surprise that I was afraid. I couldn't get the book out of my mind. And every time I thought about evil possession, I got more and more terrified. I wasn't sure that I believed in the devil, *but what if he does exist?* And then I started to become frightened of my own thoughts. *What if I attract some evil source because of my thoughts?* The fear gripped me.

Every time I tried not to think about evil, it only made me think about it more. The room was pitch dark and that made me panic all the more. The lamp was over on the other side of the room, so I couldn't just reach out to turn it on.

As I lay there frozen to my bed, I thought I heard something. *What was that?* And then I thought I felt something brush my cheek lightly. I wanted to scream out, but I couldn't speak. *Something's in my room. Someone's in my room!*

I couldn't breathe. I couldn't move. I was more terrified than I had ever been in my whole life. Then I thought I sensed movement. *What should I do?* I still couldn't move.

What if they're here to kill me? Is it a person? Or is it some evil spirit? Does it matter? Which is worse? I could maybe fight off a person. But if it's some evil entity, how could I fight that? Oh God. What am I going to do? You have to get a grip! Think. Think.

I slowly moved my arm out from under the blankets. As I lifted my hand and gently waved it around the area above me, I could feel all the hairs on my body stand on end. I quickly pulled my arm back down and shoved it under the covers. Then I thought I heard breathing close to my face. I was sure of it.

Who's there? Get out. Leave me alone. Please, just leave me alone.

But I still couldn't speak. In desperation, I called out to William in my mind. *William. Please help me. I need you.*

Nothing.

This is it. I'm going to die. I lay there, gripped in terror, for the rest of the night. And as the sunlight started to shine through the open door from the outside window, my eyes darted around the room. No one was there. Nothing was there. I felt a little relieved, but the fear was still there. And then finally, I drifted off to sleep.

A short while later, I woke to the sounds of activity upstairs in the kitchen. I immediately jumped out of bed and raced upstairs. I didn't want to be alone down there. As I ran from the room, I thought I felt someone behind me. Chasing me. And I felt the hairs on my head stand on end. But there was no one. It was just my imagination. *Or was it?*

I felt so exhausted from not sleeping the night before that I decided to turn in early that evening. My mom was still up and that made me feel more secure about going to bed. *If anything happens, she'll hear my screams. She'll come to my rescue.* I left the light on and crawled into bed.

But I couldn't sleep. The lamp didn't have a shade on it, and the light was too bright. Even when I closed my eyes, I could still see the light shining through my eyelids. I was too terrified to shut off the light, but I was also so tired. I needed to get some sleep. And I wanted to be sure to fall asleep before my mom went to bed.

Then I had an idea. I searched in the laundry room and found one of Shirley's sweaters. *That might work.* I put the sweater over top of the light bulb. There was just enough light still shining through to allow me to see, but not enough to make it hard to fall asleep.

I snuggled up under the covers and, as I lay there, I called out to William in my mind.

William. Please watch over me when I am sleeping. Please protect me. I love you. I rolled over on my side and, as I felt myself drifting off, I thought I smelled the faint hint of something burning.

As I slowly woke up, I could see that the sun was already shining brightly through the window outside my room. I rubbed my eyes and stretched. Then I suddenly realized that the light was turned off. *Maybe the bulb burned out during the night? I'll need to make sure I change it before going to bed tonight.*

I walked over to the lamp and lifted my sister's sweater off the bulb. That's when I saw it—the sweater had a huge scorch mark on it. The heat from the bulb had burnt her sweater. I reached over to the light switch and turned it on. The lamp immediately lit up. *What's going on? I know I didn't turn off the light last night. And if my mom did, she would have removed the sweater. So who turned off the light?*

I quickly hid the sweater in the laundry basket underneath some of the other clothes and ran up to the kitchen. I didn't dare ask my mom if she had been the one that turned out the light. That was the last time I'd been able to sleep without a light on.

Chapter 22

That summer turned out okay after all. I ended up hanging around with James's younger sister, Mary. She was less than a year younger than me, but she was in the grade behind me because of when her birthday fell.

I liked Mary. She was smart and fun, even if she was a little on the wild side. She was usually into drugs and heavy partying, but because she was pregnant, she drank only beer that summer. She said she couldn't stomach anything else. And I found out that she had dropped out of school when she realized she was pregnant.

Shortly after we started to hang out, I told her that I'd been pregnant, too. And then I told her about the abortion.

"I wish I had known," she said.

"Why?"

"If I'd known about you, it might have given me the courage to tell my parents. Then I could've had an abortion, too."

"At least you don't have to live with the guilt."

"I wouldn't have felt guilty. Instead, I'm stuck being pregnant all fucking summer."

I couldn't believe what she was saying. *How can she think that way while her own baby is growing inside of her? How could she not love her baby?*

It was obvious that we thought very differently on the subject, so I avoided talking to her about it anymore.

I had just gone back to school in September, when Mary had her baby. It was a boy. She said she couldn't wait to get rid of it. It! She didn't even want to see him. I had such a hard time understanding her. We got along so well, in so many ways. But this. This, I just couldn't understand.

It was only a few weeks after Mary got out of the hospital when we met the boys from out east. There were five of them and one girl, whose name was Brenda. And the guys were all hunks! All of them. In fact, you couldn't really call them boys, either. The youngest one, Jean, was six years older than me. And the oldest, Rick, was thirty-one. Brenda and Rick were together. Jean spoke French. He could speak a little English, but not really well. He pronounced his name almost like John. They had come to the big city to find work, they told us.

They were all really nice and you could tell they liked us. Even me!

So we started to hang out with them every chance we got. We spent every weekend with them, and Mary hung out with them even while I was at school. And then I started to skip school at least once a week so I could spend more time with them.

It wasn't long before Mary started to be with Paul. And I could tell that Jean was interested in me. I couldn't believe it. This gorgeous guy was actually interested in me. Me! They all seemed to have totally different taste in girls from the guys I was used to. In fact, they all treated both of us like we were really pretty. I understood them thinking that Mary was pretty, because she was. But me?

I felt so good when I was with them.

And before I knew it, I was paired off with Jean. It was great at first. I loved how he made me feel so attractive. I could tell when he looked into my eyes that he was admiring me. That he thought I was pretty.

But then I started to realize that I really had nothing in common with him. I had to admit, his broken English didn't help. But the truth was he didn't seem very bright, either. At first, it didn't matter. But eventually, I started to want more. Let's face it—we couldn't just make out all the time. As nice as that was, I really did want more. When I admitted to Mary that I was losing interest in Jean, she was amazed.

"Are you nuts?"

"I just don't have anything to talk to him about."

"Who gives a shit about talking! He's gorgeous."

"Yeah, I know. But I feel so awkward most of the time."

"Can I have him, then?"

"What about Paul?"

"He's okay. But Jean is a hunk. I'd rather have him, if you don't want him."

I couldn't believe we were having this conversation.

But when I thought about what she had suggested, I realized that I didn't really mind the idea of Mary being with Jean. And that's when I knew I shouldn't be with him anymore. "If you want him and he wants you, it's okay with me."

"Really? Are you serious? I won't make a move if you don't want me to."

I had to admit to myself that I didn't know how to break up with him. I had never had to deal with this situation before. I mean, we weren't actually girlfriend and boyfriend, not officially. He had never really asked me. But I figured I had to at least let him know that I didn't want to make out with him anymore.

And now Mary was making it easy for me. "Honest. It's okay with me."

"Do you want Paul?"

"No. That's okay. I'm really not into him."

Paul was good-looking and all, but I just wasn't attracted to him. He was too short, for one thing. And I hated the idea of being with a guy that was shorter than me.

"I know what you mean. I don't know what I ever saw in him. And besides, he's lousy in bed."

I just ignored her. *She could sound so cheap sometimes.* "It's getting late. Why don't I go home and you can talk to Jean when I'm gone." I didn't want to be there when she made her move. I was too embarrassed. *What if he doesn't want her? What if he's worried about how I would feel? What if he wants only me? What if it hurts his feelings when Mary tells him I'm not interested in him anymore?*

I found out the next day that they'd had sex the night before. *And here I was, worried about his feelings. I'm such an idiot.*

At first, over the following week, I felt a little awkward around Mary and Jean. But I soon realized they made a good pair. Somehow, she managed to bring out a whole different side of him. I discovered that he even had a good sense of humour. And Mary seemed really happy. They both did.

I was glad. But then I started to feel like a third wheel again. They always included me in all of their conversations—not like Diana. But still, whenever the rest of the guys weren't around, that uncomfortable feeling came over me. I felt like I was in the way.

Then one day, Mary told me that Rick and Brenda had broken up. And then she dropped a bombshell—Rick was interested in me!

I couldn't believe it. Rick was by far the most gorgeous of them all. I'd been attracted to him from the moment I first laid eyes on him. But he was with Brenda. And I would never go after someone who was already attached. Besides, he was so much older than me. He would never be interested in me. And he was so good-looking. *How could he ever be attracted to me?*

And now he was single. And Mary said he liked me. My head was spinning.

For the next few days, I felt shy around him and didn't know what to say. I'd always found it easy to talk to him before, but now, all of a sudden, I couldn't think of anything to say. I felt like an idiot. *What if I say the wrong thing?*

It was Rick who finally approached me. Once we started to talk, I finally relaxed. And before I knew it, I was back to feeling comfortable with him. We laughed and talked and joked around again.

But I couldn't help thinking about him in a new way, now that he was single. And now that I knew that he might be interested in me. Every night, as I lay in bed, I would imagine kissing him. I would imagine making love to him. And when we made love, everything felt perfect. He loved me and I loved him. I imagined how it would feel to finally have a boyfriend. My first boyfriend ever. I yearned to be loved. To be loved by him. I knew it was just a fantasy, but I enjoyed thinking about it. Dreaming about it. Imagining how it would feel.

So when he really kissed me for the first time, I almost passed out. I felt dizzy and I could feel my legs turn to rubber. I was in love.

But I was also afraid. Afraid that he would stop caring about me when he got to know me better. Afraid that, when we finally made love, I wouldn't know what to do. That he would realize how inexperienced I was. That he would be turned off by it. That our age difference would suddenly matter to him.

And as he continued to kiss me, passionately, I began to relax. I still worried about what he would think of me, but I felt myself sinking into the rhythm of the kiss and, before I knew it, we were both lying on the bed. *How did that happen?*

I suddenly felt self-conscious. *What if he didn't like my body? Was I too fat?*

I had always been thin, until the last few years, that is. Then I started to struggle to keep my weight down. It seemed like everything went to my hips lately. *What if he didn't like big hips?* They weren't as big as before, though. I had lost most of the weight. But not all of it.

When it finally happened, it was wonderful. It wasn't earthshattering, but I felt so close to him. I felt so loved. The feeling of connecting with another person in such an intimate way felt so special. And when it was over, he held me in his arms. And that was the best part of all. Now I really felt loved.

I moved blissfully through the next several weeks. It felt like I was living a dream. *Can this really be happening to me?* And every once in a while, I became worried that I was going to wake up and discover that it was only a dream after all.

It was Friday night and I hadn't seen Rick since Tuesday. I'd missed him so much. I couldn't wait to throw myself into his arms. As I knocked on his door, I felt my heart skip a beat at the excitement of seeing him.

But it wasn't Rick who answered the door. It was Brenda.

What's she doing here? I thought she had moved away.

"How dare you show up at my door!" she accused.

What's she talking about?

"Let me talk to her," Rick said as he came out into the hallway and pulled the door closed behind him.

What's going on? What's Brenda doing here? I don't understand?

"I'm sorry, Joanne. Brenda and I have gotten back together."

I was stunned. *How can this be happening?*

Then the door swung open and Brenda was standing there.

"Tell her the truth!" Then she looked at me. "We were never apart. I went back east to see my father when I found out he was sick. But I'm back now. So get lost! I don't ever want to see you around here again," she said, seething.

I felt like I was going to faint. I looked over at Rick and he had this look on his face. It was as if he was trying to say I'm sorry. They turned and went back into the apartment, closing the door in my face. I just stood there, staring. Stunned.

And when I finally turned and slowly walked away, I could hear laughter coming from inside the apartment.

How could I be such a fool? How could he lie to me that way? How could he use me that way? I thought he loved me. I'm such an idiot. I was just about to open the door to the stairwell when it swung open in front of me. And there was James.

"Hey, Jo. How ya doin'?"

I didn't say anything as I pushed by him.

"Hey, Jo. Stop. Talk to me. What happened?"

I started to run down the stairs. I couldn't talk to him. I couldn't admit what had happened. *What a fool I'd been.* I needed time to think. Time to figure out what I'd done. What Rick had done.

But James was right behind me. Chasing me. When he caught up to me, he grabbed my arm. "Wait, Jo. What's going on? What happened?"

He sounded so concerned. So worried. *About me? Why? Why would he care about me?*

I felt so alone. So used. So unloved. As a lone tear trickled down my face, James pulled me into his arms and held me.

I took a deep breath and told him what had happened.

"That fucking jerk. You want me to beat the shit out of him, Jo?"

Then I hesitated. I knew he would do it. James was one of the toughest guys in the neighbourhood. As tough as my brothers. Maybe even tougher. Everyone was afraid of him. Afraid to get on the wrong side of him.

"No. I just want to go home."

"You shouldn't be alone like this. Why don't you come back to my place?"

He was right. I didn't want to be alone. I didn't want to think about Rick. About what he had done to me. How he had lied to me.

So I went with James.

I sat on the side of his bed while he got me a beer.

A warm feeling washed over me as I watched him trying so hard to cheer me up.

"You know, Jo. He doesn't deserve you. You're too good for him."

But I found that hard to believe. *Nobody loves me. I don't deserve to be loved. After all, even James couldn't love me. How ironic. Here I am, listening to James, my first love, talking about how deserving I am. About how I'm too good for Rick. Well if I'm so good, then why couldn't James love me? I had loved him so hard, and for so long. And he knew it. But he couldn't love me back. So what about that? How do you explain that?*

And then he kissed me. It was a long, tender kiss. I was so confused. *Maybe this is why it happened. Maybe I needed to be free, because James had finally realized he was in love with me.*

As the tenderness of his kissing changed to passion, I started to feel excited. *He really does love me! He's always loved me. He was just too afraid to show it before. I was too young then. But I'm older now. I'm not just Kevin's little sister anymore. Now he can finally show me how much he has always loved me.*

And as he made love to me, I couldn't help thinking how glad I was that I knew what to do now. I could show him that I was all grown up now. I wasn't that little girl that still had her virginity, like the last time. When we finished, I snuggled into him and silently sighed.

This felt so right. He has always been the one. It feels as though I've been in love with him for my whole life.

"I'm sorry, Jo."

What's he talking about? Sorry for what? Oh no. Did he know? Could he tell that I didn't have an orgasm? Didn't he realize? It didn't matter. I've never had one. All that matters is that I love him. And he loves me.

"It's okay." And I snuggled in closer to him.

"No. I mean, you can't stay. I'm sorry."

I instantly froze.

"I just moved back home. My parents will kick me out if they find you here. You have to go."

And then something snapped inside of me. *It doesn't matter. Nothing matters anymore. I am nothing. Nobody.*

I didn't say a word. I got up and put my clothes on. I grabbed my coat and walked out the door to the stairs. And as I walked up the stairs, I thought I heard him whisper, "Wait, Jo. I'm sorry. You understand, don't you?" But I couldn't be sure. It didn't matter anyway. Nothing mattered.

The pain was like no other. I had never felt such despair before. Reality was setting in. *The only two men I've ever loved have used me. They never loved me at all. How could they? I'm not worthy of their love. I don't deserve their love. I don't deserve anyone's love. I am worthless. My life means nothing.*

And as I walked the rest of the way home, I made the decision. I went up the stairs and into the bathroom. I opened the medicine cabinet and found what I was looking for. *Good.* The bottle was almost full. Close to five hundred aspirins. *That should do it.* I took them out and filled the glass with water.

As I filled my palm and threw the pills in my mouth, I couldn't help thinking about all the times I had swallowed my vegetables whole. It was as if, somehow, I'd been preparing for this very night. I gulped them down and poured another handful out. When the bottle was almost empty, I stopped. I wanted to leave a small amount. I didn't want anyone to know what I had done.

I went down to my room in the basement, got into bed, and waited. While I was lying there, I started to think about Rick again. And James. Suddenly, my emotional numbness changed back to the deep despair I'd been feeling earlier. The tears poured down my face as I thought about the horrible, worthless person I had become.

It won't be long now. Soon the pain will be gone. Soon I will be gone. Please, just let me go to sleep and never wake up. And then I thought about afterward. When they found me. Dead. *How will Rick and James feel then? Maybe I should write a note. Maybe then, they'll understand the pain they caused me. Let them live with that the rest of their lives.*

No! I can't do that. My despair had turned to anger. *I could never let them know how much pain they've caused me. That will only make me seem weak. But I am weak. But I can't let them know. Why should I give them the satisfaction of knowing how much control they had over me? They don't deserve to know!*

And with the anger, I suddenly realized, *I don't want to die!* But it was too late. It felt like the room was spinning. My eyelids grew heavy. I could barely keep my eyes open. I was falling asleep. It was happening. I could feel it, but I couldn't stop it.

As I found myself finally giving in to the permanent slumber of death, I began to have a pleasant thought. *At least I'll be with William again. Forever.* And when I thought about William, a feeling of peace and overwhelming love washed over me. And that's how I was feeling, as I drifted into a deep, deep sleep.

Joanne. Wake up. You must wake up.

I felt something jolting me awake.

This isn't your time, dear child.

William? Is that you?

Get up, little one. You have a big life ahead of you. But you must get up. Now!

As I became fully awake, I understood the urgency of their words. When I jumped out of bed, it felt like the room was spinning out of control. I stumbled into the laundry room and got to the sink just in time.

I kept retching and retching, throwing up everything in my stomach. When I thought it was finally over, I raised my head and the room started spinning again. I leaned over the sink and threw up some more. I could feel my throat burning and it became painful to throw up. But I couldn't stop. Every time I thought it was over, I would start heaving again. I had never felt so sick in all my life.

Eventually, after more than an hour, I stopped throwing up. There was simply nothing left. But that didn't stop the heaving. I picked up the jug we always used when someone was sick. My brothers used to call it the puke jug, and the name stuck. So with the puke jug held tightly in my arms, I went back to bed.

I felt dizzy and weak. I was feeling so sick that it didn't occur to me to be afraid—afraid that I hadn't gotten rid of all the drugs from my body. Eventually, I drifted off to sleep. But then the heaving would start again, and it would wake me up.

By the time morning arrived, I had spent a fitful night going in and out of sleep. And heaving without any results. I still felt really sick, but not nearly as bad as the night before. As I started to feel a little better, the fear began to creep up on me. *What if I'm still going to die? What if I didn't get all the drugs out?* I still felt dizzy and sick, which only added to my fear. *If I got it all out, I wouldn't still be feeling so sick. Would I? How can I get Mom to help me without letting her know what I did? I have to think of something. Something she'll believe.*

When I finally went up to the kitchen, I had an idea.

"You look like shit!" she said immediately.

"I'm sick," I said. And then I started to cry.

"Were you drinking last night?"

"No. I didn't have anything to drink," I lied. *It's not a big lie. I only had one beer at James's place.*

"I think I have food poisoning."

"How did you get food poisoning?"

"I had a hamburger at the diner. It must have been bad." And just as I finished answering her, I jumped up and ran to the sink. I was heaving uncontrollably, but nothing came up. When I finally finished, I looked over at my mom again. As she stared at me, I saw her face change to fear.

"You look green. I need to call the hospital. I need to find out what we should do." As she talked on the phone, I started to get more and more scared. Her reaction scared me. I could see the fear in her face and hear the fear in her voice. *What if it's too late? What if they can't do anything for me? What if I'm going to die after all?*

My fear grew into terror. *I don't want to die. I want to live. Please let me be okay.*

When my mom got off the phone, she told me they said I would probably be alright. That I had probably gotten it all out of me. "But they said I'll need to keep an eye on you for the next couple of days."

That's fine with me. I didn't want to be alone. *And maybe she'll let me sleep with her tonight.*

"They said you're probably going to feel sick for at least a few days. They said it will take that long to get it completely out of your system."

I felt so relieved. I still felt really sick, but now it didn't scare me. I figured that poisoning must be pretty close to overdosing, so I was reassured when they had said it was normal to still feel sick. And they'd been right. After three days, I started to feel a lot better. I still felt weak, but that was probably because I could barely eat anything. About the only thing I could stomach was dry soda crackers.

Looking back later, I realized it had been a blessing that I felt so sick for those first few weeks after. While I was feeling that sick, I didn't once think about Rick or James. It gave me the time I needed to accept what had happened. To accept what they had both done to me. And how I had let it happen.

Then finally, when I was feeling more myself again, I thought about William. I thought about how they had saved my life. And then

I remembered my sister's burnt sweater. I thought about how someone had turned off the light that night. Had it been William? Had William saved my life twice? *It doesn't matter. I know for sure they saved my life that one night. That's all that matters.*

And as I thought about William and what they had done for me, this feeling of incredible gratitude washed over me. I felt so thankful to have William in my life—a life that wouldn't even exist today if it hadn't been for William.

Thank you, William. I love you so much.

Chapter 23

I didn't see much of Mary over the next couple of months. She was still going around with Jean and I didn't want to run into Rick, so I kept away from them. Diana was all wrapped up with her latest boyfriend, so I started spending more time with my friend Jane.

Jane was very outgoing and I enjoyed her company. It was a really nice change. Jane was still a virgin, which I found very refreshing, too. I liked that she was still so inexperienced and innocent. It finally felt like my life was turning around.

*

It was Saturday night and we were going over to visit one of Jane's friends, Gail. She didn't live near us, or even go to the same school, so I had never met her before. Jane had met Gail one time when she was visiting her grandmother. And they had been close friends ever since. She told me she tried to visit Gail as often as she could.

When we arrived at Gail's house, I discovered that her older brother Mike and his friend Pete were also there. Mike and Pete were only a year older than us. They seemed really nice and so we all hung out together. We laughed and joked around and had a really nice time. Later in the evening, Jane admitted to me and Gail that she was really attracted to Pete.

"Do you think he likes me?" she asked Gail.

"I think he might. He seems to be spending a lot of time with you. He never shows me that much attention."

"What should I do?"

"Why don't you tell him how you feel?"

"I'm too nervous. I wouldn't know what to say. Can you tell him for me?"

"Sure."

I was actually feeling nervous for Jane. *I hope he likes her.* He seemed like such a nice guy. And cute. They both were. In fact, I thought Mike was even more attractive than Pete, but not by much.

Once Gail went back in the other room to talk to Pete, Jane got herself into a real state. She was both excited and nervous at the same time. I kept trying to reassure her, and reminded her of what Gail had said.

"He must like you. Gail said he never shows this much interest in her. And look at Gail—she's beautiful."

"I know. But what if she's wrong? What if he's just being nice?"

"Just relax, Jane. You'll know the answer in a few minutes."

"That's what I'm afraid of."

"I'm sure he likes you. Don't worry. Just take a deep breath."

And then Gail came running back into the room where we were waiting. "He likes you! I knew it. He wants to go out on a date with you next Saturday." She had to pause after every few words to catch her breath. I was so thrilled for Jane. All three of us got so caught up in the excitement that we forgot they were in the next room.

"What's all the commotion in here?" Mike asked, as he came in the room.

Jane looked so embarrassed.

"Nothing." I answered quickly. "We were just joking around."

"So I hear that Jane and Pete are going out on a date next Saturday." He was looking right at me.

My heart skipped a beat. *Why is he talking directly to me? Why isn't he looking at Jane? Why is he blushing? Do I make him nervous? Why?*

"Umm, I was thinking. Would you like to make it a double date?"

He's talking to me! He's actually asking me out. On a date. Me! No one has ever asked me out on a date before. This is how normal people do it. And then I realized that he was starting to look rejected, as I was taking so long to answer.

"Sure, that would be nice."

He smiled and looked relieved.

I still couldn't believe it. And Jane was thrilled that we would be going, too.

     *

The following Saturday was amazing. They took us out to dinner and then to a movie. It was just like a real date was supposed to be. And when the evening was over, he didn't even try to make out with me. I had worried periodically throughout the date about how I would handle it if he came on to me. But instead, he leaned over and gave me a quick, gentle kiss on the lips and told me that he'd had a really nice time. *He'd had a really nice time!* And then he asked me if I would like to go out with him again next Friday. I was thrilled.

Over the next few weekends, we continued to double date with Jane and Pete. Our kissing had increased to necking, but he still hadn't made a move to do anything but kiss. I was relieved and frustrated, all at the same time.

Then finally, on our fourth weekend of dating, he asked me to be his steady girlfriend. I was stunned. And thrilled. I finally had a boyfriend. A real boyfriend. My very first boyfriend, ever. And we still hadn't done anything but kiss. *He's interested in me! Not just my body. So this is what it feels like to have a real boyfriend?* I liked it. No—I loved it.

We'd been going steady for several more weeks and we still hadn't done anything more than kissing and a little petting. I'd gotten so excited during some of our heavy petting, but thankfully, he had more control than I was used to. I wanted him so badly, but I was also glad we were taking it slow. I knew if he had tried to go further, I would have let him. So I was happy he hadn't tried yet.

Jane and Pete were still going strong, too. Jane told me one day that she thought she was falling in love with him. And that made me think about Mike. *Do I love him? Am I in love with him?* I knew I cared very deeply for him. And I also knew that I was extremely attracted to him. *But do I love him?* I suddenly realized that didn't trust my judgment anymore. I knew it had failed me in the past.

Or had it? Just because they hadn't loved me back, doesn't mean that the love wasn't real for me. I was wrong in believing that they loved me, too. I know that now. But does that mean I was wrong to love them? I realized I shouldn't let my past influence my ability to love now. And as that realization sank in, I had to admit that I had fallen in love with Mike. He wasn't like anyone I had ever been with before. And I could tell that he cared about me, too.

So when Jane announced that she and Pete were going away the next weekend and asked if Mike and I wanted to come too, I blurted out, yes. She went on to explain that she wanted to give her virginity to Pete and that they were planning a romantic weekend away in Niagara Falls.

I wasn't sure how I was going to suggest it to Mike, but I didn't have to. Jane told Pete and Pete told Mike. So before I knew it, we were all planning this amazing, romantic getaway.

The whole weekend was wonderful. The four of us had so much fun together and when we paired off to go to our rooms, it was the most incredible experience I had ever had. I really was in love with Mike.

A few weeks later, it was coming up to New Year's Eve. I was so excited to finally have a boyfriend to celebrate New Year's with. My mom was going down to Grandma's cottage with her boyfriend and my sister Shirley. Carol had moved out a while back, so I was going to have the house all to myself. Jane and I had planned everything. It was going to be just the four of us. I prepared snacks and got someone to buy us beer. Then Jane and I got all dressed up for the big night.

And it was everything I imagined it would be. We talked and laughed and listened to music. Then, when the slow songs came on the radio, we all danced. It felt so good to slow dance with Mike. It was romantic and seductive, all at the same time. It was the perfect night to bring in the New Year. I thought it was a good sign. *This is a good omen.* My life had finally turned itself around and I believed that everything was going to be alright. Better than alright. *This next year is going to be my best ever.* I just knew it.

It was the middle of January when Jane called me on the phone in a panic. Pete had broken up with her and she didn't know what to do.

"I love him so much, Jo. I just can't bear the thought of living without him. What am I going to do?"

Then I remembered Rick and James. And that night. I knew exactly how Jane was feeling. I also knew that there was very little I could say to make her feel better. But that didn't stop me from trying. We talked for over an hour and, in the end, I was pretty sure she sounded better. Not much, but definitely a little.

Once I got off the phone, I started to worry. *What if Mike wants to break up with me, too?* We had always spent so much time double dating. *What if he only wanted to be with me as long as Pete was with Jane?* So I tried to brace myself for the possibility that Mike was going to call me and break up. At first, when I didn't hear from him, I was relieved. But when I didn't hear from him all night, I got worried. And then I started to dread his phone call.

By the time I finally heard from him, I was convinced that he didn't want to go steady with me anymore. But instead, he admitted that he had delayed calling me because he was ashamed of what Pete had done to Jane.

I was so relieved. And then I got mad at myself. *Why did I have to doubt myself? Why did I immediately assume the worst? I need to work on that.*

*

The rest of the winter flew by. Mike and I spent every weekend together. Jane was still depressed about Pete, but she was finally starting to sound a little better. We talked on the phone every couple of days, but I didn't see much of her. She kept saying that she preferred to stay close to home. She wasn't in the mood for socializing. I felt bad for her. I knew what she was going through, and I also knew that she needed time to get over him.

Then one Thursday evening, I answered the phone and it was Mike. He sounded strange. I couldn't quite put my finger on it, but something was wrong. I was immediately on alert. He kept going on and on about his ex-girlfriend and how he had never really truly gotten over her. And then he said it. He was getting back with her. She said she wanted to get back with him and he needed to try to make it work. He said he couldn't give me his whole heart as long as he still had feelings for her.

I was numb. I could barely speak. So instead, I just listened. At the end of the conversation, he apologized and asked if we could still be friends. He said he really cared about me, but he had to do this. He had to try one more time with her. I didn't know what to say, so I said, yes.

I knew I didn't want it to be over. So I thought that as long as we were still friends, maybe there was a chance we might get back together. But I didn't truly believe that either. I just couldn't break off our relationship completely, all at once. I couldn't accept the finality of it. I needed to cling to the possibility that we might be together again.

As I sat in my room thinking over the conversation with Mike, I was tempted to talk to William about it. After all, I had spent my whole life relying on William to explain things to me. To make me feel better.

But lately, I had started to doubt William. To doubt their very existence. I had started to wonder if they were just a child's imaginary friends. And when I thought that way, it made me feel lonely. I didn't like it. But I wasn't a little kid anymore. And then I thought about the time they saved my life. *They have to be real. Don't they? But what if it was just me? What if I was the one that woke myself up that night? What if I was the one who turned off the light that other night?*

And then I thought about all the lessons they had taught me. *They must be real. How could I possibly know all those things at such a young age? How could I possibly be so wise? Even Mom had been shocked at some of the things I knew. They have to be real. But what if they're not?* I realized I hadn't talked to William in such a long time, and my doubts increased. I was growing up, and my connection with them was fading away. I didn't want to think about it, so I pushed it out of my mind.

But as I fell asleep that night, my thoughts weren't on my breakup with Mike. They were on William. And that's when I realized that I was more upset about the loss of William than about the loss of Mike.

I woke up the next morning feeling so alone. So depressed. I thought about Rick again, and all the old feelings resurfaced about being used. Then I thought about James, and I felt the pain sear through me. I needed to shake myself out of this depression. *Why do I keep going back over the same painful memories? Why can't I let them go?*

And then, over the next few weeks, my whole life changed. A few days after Mike and I broke up, my mom announced we were moving. She had bought a house in a small town near my grandma's cottage. Now all she had to do was sell this house.

At first, I was in a panic. But then I started to think. *Maybe it's the best thing that could happen to me. It will give me a fresh start. I can leave all my bad memories behind me. I can start a new life in a new town—a place where nobody knows me.*

Our house sold quickly. Mom said she got more than her asking price for it. She was thrilled. Her boyfriend Gordon was moving down with us. He'd been living with Mom for a couple of years now, so it was no surprise. He was nice. But not like Carl. No one was like Carl.

It still stung when I thought about him. I missed him. But I was also angry with him. And then I would feel so lonely. So abandoned. I never quite got over the fact that he didn't call me. He never contacted me again. *How can someone say they love you and then just abandon you that way?* As moving day fast approached, I got more and more excited.

Mike had phoned me a few times. But every time he called, he managed to bring up his girlfriend, which annoyed me. But I didn't say anything. It didn't matter. I was moving. We wouldn't have been able to continue our relationship anyway.

Then finally, the day arrived. I left my old life behind, and embarked on a new adventure.

Chapter 24

I slowly opened my eyes and adjusted to the beautiful orange glow of the rising sun beaming in the window of my new bedroom. As I became fully awake, I realized I must have fallen asleep shortly after one o'clock in the morning. That was the last time I had checked my clock. I reached over and shut off my bedside lamp. I glanced at the clock. It was still early. I didn't have to get up yet.

My excitement was building. Today was going to be the first day at my new school. I'd made a decision during the night. I was going to focus on my studies. I was going to work really hard and finish high school. Then I would go on to university, to study law. *I'm going to be a lawyer!*

I knew I could do it. I was smart. I had always done well in school, even without trying. I had a great memory and I seemed to learn easily. My mom had always said I was really smart and could do anything I wanted to do, be anything I wanted to be. *And I want to be a lawyer.*

As a lawyer, people will respect me. People will look up to me. I will be a professional. They will have to respect me. But I've always wanted to be a writer, too. I want to write books. I've always loved to write. I write all the time. But what if I'm not good enough? What if nobody wants to read my books?

Don't do that. Don't doubt yourself. Of course people will want to read your books. But what about being a lawyer? I really want to be a lawyer too.

I can do both. Lots of people do both. In fact, most of the authors of the books I've read were something else as well as being an author. Yes, that's it. I'm going to be a lawyer and a writer. When I go to school today, I'll make sure I'm able to take extra classes in English Literature. And they might even have a creative writing course.

Then I started to panic. *What if I can't do it? What if this school is harder than my old school? And even worse, what if no one likes me? What if nothing has changed? What if I just brought my old, miserable life with me?*

Stop it! You can't think that way. What did William always say?

William. I felt the tears well up in my eyes. *How could I ever survive without William? Don't be silly. William isn't real!* But even as the thought burst out in my mind, I started to feel sick to my stomach. *They had to be real.*

And then I thought back again. To the time I stole the chocolate bars. And about my dad. William had made me feel loved when felt I didn't deserve anyone's love. I thought about all the times I'd felt lost. When I felt so lonely and unworthy. I thought about that time when I gave in to my despair. *No, don't go there. Yes, go there! William was there. William saved me.*

And the pain of my loss gripped me again. *Why can't I let go? Why can't I just accept that they weren't real?* My head knew that they couldn't be real. But my heart thought differently.

I thought about all the lessons I had learned from them and I smiled. But the tears kept flowing. *How could I ever doubt William? How could I think they weren't real? They had taught me so much.*

Get a grip! They were just a figment of your imagination. You needed them, so you created them. They weren't real!

But I couldn't bear that thought. Every time I thought of them as being unreal, I got this sick feeling—this gut-wrenching pain and emptiness that I could feel down to the core of my being.

And as the tears flowed freely down my face, I cried out in my mind, *I'm sorry, William.* I knew it was my fault they were gone. They hadn't abandoned me. I had abandoned them. *I want to believe in you. I really do.* And I meant it.

Please, William. Show me that you're real. I want you to be real. But they weren't there. I couldn't feel them. I couldn't hear them. I felt so alone without William. So weak. So out of control. But I had to go on. I had to make this life of mine count. This was my second chance. The chance William gave me. I couldn't help myself. I had to acknowledge it. William had saved my life.

As I rose from my bed that morning, I was still feeling the agony of loss. And I grieved for that loss. *But wait. They don't have to be gone. I'm the one who deserted them and I'm the one who can bring them back. Of course they're real. How could they not be real? I love them and they love me. And I know that their love is real.*

I immediately noticed, as I thought about William being real, that familiar warmth washing over me. *How could I possibly think that William was ever really gone? They were always with me. Watching over me. Guiding me. They were part of me and I was part of them.*

Hello, luv.

William! You're back.

We are always with you dear one. You know that.

Yes I do.

We can feel that you do.

The tears were pouring down my face, but I wasn't sad. They were tears of joy. And relief.

I'm sorry for doubting you. For losing faith.

That is not important. Your joy and love are all that matter.

When I believe in you, I feel joy. But when I didn't believe in you, I felt lost, alone and in pain.

Let that be your guide, dear one. Let us be your guide.

What do you mean?

Your emotions will tell you whether your thoughts are similar to ours or not. We only want joy and love and excitement in your life. And we will always guide you to that. If your thoughts do not lead you to those emotions, then you must choose to change your thoughts.

I thought back over the things I had been thinking and how my emotions kept changing, based on what I had been thinking at any given moment. I was finally starting to understand. *I have control over my thoughts. And if I have control over my thoughts, then I ultimately have control over my feelings. That means that I have the potential to be happy all the time, if I choose to be.* An incredible thrill washed over me.

We are very pleased. You have come a long way, dear one. We feel the excitement of your growth.

And then I felt their joy and love filling me with the most exhilarating feeling I had ever felt before. The feeling of love was more incredible than words could describe. It was soft, warm, gentle and soothing, while at the same time strong, intense, powerful and complete.

And as I basked in their love for me, the tears of joy flowing freely, I dropped down to my knees and called out in my mind, *I love you, William. I love you so much. I'll never doubt you again.*

Chapter 25

As I walked out of the house that morning, I felt the excitement, the eagerness, the anticipation of embarking on the first day of the rest of my life. And when my new school came into sight, I could still feel the warm glow of William permeating me as I heard their loving words sing out and echo down to the very depths of my soul.

Our love for you is greater than you know.

The End

www.ingramcontent.com/pod-product-compliance
Lightning Source LLC
La Vergne TN
LVHW011225080426
835509LV00005B/327